MANIPUR DIARIES

Stories from India's Hidden Heartland

AISHWARYA VIKRAM NADHE

LAUNCHPAD

An imprint of
Srishti Publishers & Distributors

Srishti Publishers & Distributors
A unit of AJR Publishing LLP
212A, Peacock Lane
Shahpur Jat, New Delhi – 110 049
editorial@srishtipublishers.com

First published by Launchpad,
an imprint of Srishti Publishers & Distributors in 2025

10 9 8 7 6 5 4 3 2 1

Contents

Prologue

Manipur Diaries is a journey of self-transformation that intertwines the natural beauty, diverse cuisines, rich culture, and history of Manipur. This book is more than just a travel narrative; it is a genuine expression of appreciation for Manipur's beauty, culture, and way of life. Through Gatha's perspective, readers are invited to explore many beautiful places of Manipur, savour the diverse flavours of its cuisine, experience traditional music, dance, and art, celebrate its festivals, and hear the whispers of a land steeped in tradition and vitality.

This book follows Gatha, a travel journalist from Pune, who is assigned to explore the untapped tourism potential of Manipur for the Incredible India Travel and Tourism Magazine. Hesitant at first, she embarks on what she perceives as just another routine assignment. However, her journey quickly transforms into an adventure of self-discovery as she uncovers the stories and mysteries concealed within Manipur's tranquil landscapes, unexplored places, ancient traditions, and the lives of its people. Along her journey, she forms bonds with many individuals, including fishermen, Imas, storytellers, and guides, feeling an unexpected connection with them. She also encounters legends passed down through generations, unveiling the deep bond between the land and its cultural heritage. The land is not just a destination she stumbled upon; it is a place that called to her softly, insistently, like a whisper on the edge of a dream—a whisper that promised adventure, wonder, and perhaps, a piece of herself.

For Gatha, a city-bound journalist jaded by routine and noise, Manipur was never on radar. But fate has a curious way of reshaping maps and lives. What started as a professional duty soon became something deeply personal. The quiet strength of the Manipuri people and their unspoken resilience, shaped by history, began to mirror her own inner struggles. From the lively Ima Keithel, Asia's largest all-women market, where generations of women have held the economy together, to the enchanting beauty of Loktak Lake—the largest freshwater lake in Northeast India and the only place in the world with floating *phumdis*—every encounter stirs something deep within her.

She finds herself captivated by the precision of the polo game, moved by the spiritual depth of the *Ras Leela* performances, intrigued by lotus silk, and lost in the oral histories of the region. Each place she visits has a unique rhythm, some echoing with songs while others resonate with the beats of vibrant festivals bursting into life.

As she treks through the mystic hills of Ukhrul, explores the sacred caves of Tamenglong, savours the different flavours of Manipur, learns about its dance, music, art, and culture, listens to elders recount folktales by firelight, and observes young artisans preserving age-old crafts with quiet pride, she finds herself drawn into a rhythm of life that is slow, intentional, and deeply rooted. She begins documenting more than just tourist attractions; she captures the soul of Manipur through unexplored places and forgotten legends.

Each step of her journey unfolds like a chapter in a forgotten manuscript. All the fragments come together to form a mosaic of experiences that shift something within her. In Manipur's timeless silence and vibrant traditions, she begins to listen to the whisperings of her own heart, something she had long silenced beneath the pressures of deadlines.

By the time her assignment comes to an end, she realizes that her story has become deeply intertwined with Manipur. She had arrived to write about a place but ended up being rewritten by it—her notes were no longer just an article; they had transformed into reflections, confessions, and love letters to a land that held up a mirror to her soul.

Manipur—'The Jewel Land'—with its rich tapestry of places, food, and culture, forever changes her perception of the world. She had come looking for a feature story but instead found herself woven into the very fabric of the place.

When she finally leaves Manipur, weeks after her planned departure, she carries more than just photographs, sketches, and notes. She carries whispers of resilience, identity, and connection. She carries a new understanding of herself, one that has been quietly shaped by the land and its people.

And so, *Manipur Diaries* was born—not as an article, but as a tribute. A journey. A remembrance. Because some places don't just change your view; they change you.

Key Characters

- **Gatha:** A curious but sceptical traveller who arrives in Manipur with little understanding of the region. Her journey transforms her and shifts her perspective significantly, leading her to appreciate the beauty and traditions of the region.

- **Thambal**: A passionate guide and environmentalist who introduces Gatha to the secrets of Manipur. His deep knowledge and love for his homeland inspire Gatha throughout the journey.

- **Pujari:** A serene and devout priest from the Shree Govindajee Temple who shares the spiritual essence and origins of the temple.

- **Imas of the Market:** The strong, entrepreneurial mothers of the Keithel (Market), who represent female empowerment, and tradition, as well as embody the heartbeat of Manipuri society.

- **Ireima:** A skilled craftswoman from Andro Village, devoted to the ancient art of pottery. Through her hands and stories, she reveals the deep cultural significance of clay work in Andro, blending tradition with quiet resilience.

- **Fisherman:** A quiet yet wise man from Thanga Island who lives harmoniously with nature, sharing ancient tales and the delicate balance required to protect the phumdis (floating islands) of Loktak Lake.

- **Leima:** An elderly woman who had lived through the struggles and challenges of the INA movement and witnessed firsthand the impact of the Japanese occupation in Manipur. She resides in a modest home on the outskirts of Moirang and offers poignant memories of wartime resilience and hope.

- **Shanngam:** Upon arriving in Ukhrul, Gatha and Thambal are welcomed by Shanngam, a respected elder who shares the tribe's stories, customs, and deep-rooted connection with the land.

- **Sana:** A local youth who becomes their guide through the mystical Mova Cave, unveiling legends, and hidden corners of Manipur's ancient landscapes.

- **Curator:** The guardians of history who preserve and narrate Manipur's past, from war relics to folk traditions, with pride and depth.

- **Thonglen:** A lively and joyful boy from Churachandpur, seen skipping stones in the dam water with his friends. His playful energy and connection to the land reflect the pride of the younger generation growing up in harmony with their surroundings.

- **Villagers from different villages:** Each village offers a unique lens into the state's rich tapestry, showcasing festivals, agriculture, crafts, or community life, highlighting unity in diversity.

- **Vendors from different markets:** Diverse voices and faces, each representing a region of Manipur, sharing flavours, crafts, and tales that reflect the rich cultural mosaic of the state.

- **Waiter of Luxmi Kitchen:** An everyday hero who offers not just food but also stories, smiles, and slices of local life in one of Imphal's beloved eateries.

- **Artisans of Manipur:** The weavers, potters, woodworkers, cane-workers, painters, and performers whose craftsmanship preserves traditions across generations.

- **People of Manipur:** The soul of the story—resilient, welcoming, proud, and deeply rooted in their land, culture, and identity.

I

THE BEGINNING – A HESITANT JOURNEY

The early morning flight touched down at Imphal Airport, the sun casting a golden hue over the lush green hills surrounding the capital of Manipur. Gatha stretched her cramped legs, her leather tote bag slung over one shoulder, and looked around. A sudden wave of nausea washed over her; this was a far cry from the urban chaos of Pune that she was accustomed to. The airport was smaller, the air fresher, and the sky seemed impossibly blue.

Thambal, a lean man in his late twenties with fair skin and an infectious smile, was waiting for her near the arrivals gate. Dressed in a simple shirt with a shawl draped over his shoulders, he waved enthusiastically when he spotted her.

"You must be Gatha! Welcome to Manipur!" he greeted her warmly. His accent was musical, his tone inviting.

"Thank you," she replied hesitantly, unsure of how she would adjust to the tranquil serenity of this place.

Gatha's journey began in Imphal, the capital of Manipur, a city alive with stories and culture. As they drove through the city, Gatha gazed out of the car window. The streets were lined with wooden houses painted in soft hues of blue and green, their porches adorned with colourful flowerpots. People walked leisurely, and the honking of vehicles was rare, almost subdued—a stark contrast to the relentless pace of Pune.

"You will be staying at this hotel tonight," Thambal said. "Hotel Imphal is among the best hotels in the city. All the arrangements have been made for you. You relax for a while, and then we will head to our first destination, Kangla Fort."

Hotel Imphal is an excellent choice for travellers visiting Imphal, offering a serene environment along with many useful amenities designed to enhance your experience.

Gatha felt a bit tired and freshened up before having lunch. After relaxing for a while, she began her journey towards her first destination with Thambal. She was still trying to grasp the nuances of this new place and was captivated by her surroundings.

"First Stop: Kangla Fort," Thambal announced, glancing at her. "This place is the heart of Manipur's history."

Kangla Fort: A Step into the Past

The entrance to Kangla Fort was immense and majestic. Thambal parked the car, and Gatha stepped out, her eyes tracing the imposing statue that had stood as a silent witness to Manipur's history. Thambal handed her a bottle of water. She took a sip, her gaze settling on the arched gateway ahead, where the past seemed to whisper through the rustling leaves of the sacred trees within.

Thambal adjusted his bag, mobile in hand, and said, "Welcome to the heart of Manipuri legacy."

Taking a deep breath, she stepped forward, ready to walk through history.

"The word 'Kangla' means 'dry land' in the old Meitei language," Thambal explained. "This gate is known as Kangla Sanathong, which translates to 'The Royal Entrance to Kangla' in Meitei," he added. "The entrance is flanked by a statue of Meidingu Nara Singh, also known as Maharaja Narasingh. He was a king who fiercely defended the motherland and always prioritized the welfare of the people over the powers he possessed as a ruler," he said.

As Gatha followed him, she felt a strange calmness wash over her as they wandered past ancient temples, crumbling walls, and tranquil water bodies. They first stopped at the massive white statues of Kangla Sha, the mythical dragon lions, their detailed carvings showcasing the skills of Manipuri craftsmen.

Gesturing towards these dragon lions, Thambal explained, "The fort housed important structures like this one, the Kangla Sha, which symbolizes royal power. These mythical creatures represent royal authority and protection. Traditionally, two large dragon statues guard the entrance, embodying power and spirituality. The sculptures are intricately designed, blending indigenous art with mythological symbolism."

Gatha stood in awe for a few minutes, mesmerized by the beauty of these statues.

"This seems magical," she exclaimed in amazement.

Continuing their tour, they arrived at the inner sanctum where the Coronation Hall, known as Uttra, stood. Its architecture was simple yet impressive, a testament to the power and humility of the Manipuri kings.

"This fort was once the seat of the Manipur kingdom," Thambal explained as they walked through the wide gates. "It dates back to the pre-colonial era, and its history is intertwined with the region's identity. Originally established by the Ningthouja dynasty, it grew into a powerful kingdom under rulers like Maharaja Gharib Niwaj (1709-1748), who expanded its territory."

Gatha listened intently, her footsteps echoing on the ancient pathway. The fort's expansive grounds stretched before them, marked by the remains of old temples and sacred sites.

"It was the political and spiritual centre of the Meitei rulers," Thambal continued, gesturing toward the remains of the Coronation Hall. "For centuries, Kangla was a symbol of power—until the British seized it. The fort was taken over by the British after the Anglo-Manipur War of 1891, following the execution of Prince Tikendrajit and other Manipuri leaders."

Her fingertips brushed against the aged stone of a nearby structure.

"This fort has seen so many sacrifices," she said, feeling the weight of history embedded in the surface of the stone.

"Did you know that a large portion of this fort was demolished by the British during their rule?" Thambal asked, his voice tinged with sadness. "However, it represents perseverance. The Manipuri people have rebuilt parts of it, preserving our heritage and legacy. Kangla holds a sacred status among the Meitei as it is thought to be the dwelling place of their deity, Pakhangba."

"And hence the fort still stands," she mused.

Gatha scribbled notes in her journal. Despite her initial reluctance, she felt a growing curiosity about this land and its stories. She began noting down key architectural features in her journal as she followed Thambal to the important structures. Then, they walked towards the Govindajee Temple inside the Kangla Fort.

"This is built in traditional Meitei style, which is influenced by Hindu architecture," he said. "It is dedicated to Lord Govindajee, a form of Krishna, reflecting the influence of Vaishnavism in Manipur. The temple showcases a raised base, slanted roofs, and intricate sculptures."

They stood there for some time, took blessings, and then left for the southern courtyard, where a lone banyan tree stood. Its gnarled roots gripped the earth like the memories of a forgotten past.

"This tree has witnessed it all," Thambal said, pausing beneath its vast canopy. "Legends say that the kings once meditated here before making important decisions."

A soft breeze rustled the leaves, as if echoing the whispered prayers of rulers long gone. Gatha traced a fallen leaf between her fingers.

"So much has happened here," she murmured, her voice filled with amazement.

Thambal nodded. "Kangla is more than a place—it's a spirit, one that refuses to be erased. It remains a symbol of Manipuri identity, resistance, and resilience."

Gatha closed her journal for a moment, letting the weight of his words settle in. The fort was no longer just a historical site to her; it was proof of survival, a living memory etched into the land itself.

Ima Keithel: The Women's Market

By mid-afternoon, they arrived at 'Ima Keithel', the renowned 'Mother's Market'. 'Ima' means 'mother' in the Manipuri language. The air buzzed with energy, the rows of stalls manned solely by women. The market was a rainbow of colours—vibrant woven shawls, sparkling jewellery, fresh vegetables, and aromatic spices were all on display. One could find almost anything and everything in one place.

"This is one of the oldest and largest women-run markets in the world," Thambal said with pride. "It is more than just a marketplace; it is a symbol of women's empowerment in Manipur."

As they wandered through the bustling lanes, the rhythmic chatter of women bargaining, the clinking of brassware, and the rustling of handwoven textiles filled the air. The scent of fresh herbs blended with the rich aroma of dried fish and traditional sweets, creating a sensory tapestry unique to Ima Keithel. Elderly vendors, faces lined with wisdom, sat gracefully behind neatly arranged goods, while younger women skilfully attended to customers with practised ease. Every corner of the market seemed to tell a story of resilience, tradition, and an unbroken legacy passed down through generations. Watching the vibrant scene unfold, they felt the heartbeat of Manipur, alive in the voices, and spirit of the women who had shaped this historic marketplace.

Gatha wandered through the lanes, amazed by the women's entrepreneurial spirit. An elderly lady with a weathered face and sparkling eyes waved her over, showcasing a basket of handwoven scarves and *phaneks*.

"These are phaneks, the traditional Manipuri sarongs," Thambal translated as the woman spoke in the Manipuri language. "She says you should try one."

Gatha hesitated but then ran her fingers over the fabric, admiring the unique and detailed patterns woven with care.

"This is beautiful. I have never seen such unique designs and patterns," she said.

The phanek felt soft yet sturdy. Smiling, she picked up a red one with black embroidery. The elderly woman gestured for Gatha to wrap it around her waist. She adjusted it, feeling an unexpected connection to the culture. Around her, the market pulsed with life. Gatha caught her reflection in a mirror propped up against a stall and smiled. In that moment, she didn't just feel like a visitor; she felt like she belonged here.

As they moved through the market, she sampled local snacks. Each bite of those delicacies was an explosion of flavours, unlike anything she had tasted before. The *eromba*, with its bold mix of mashed vegetables, fermented fish, and fiery chillies, left a pleasant warmth on her tongue. The *singju* (a local traditional salad made of fresh green herbs, lotus stems, soaked dried peas, fermented fish, king chilli, perilla seeds also known as black sesame, chickpea powder, and roasted gram flour) and *bora* (a local fried vegetable snack, also known as *pakoda*) lingered long after the last bite. The crispiness of the *bora*, deep-fried to golden perfection, contrasted beautifully with the refreshing crunch of the *singju*, bursting with flavour. Gatha savoured every mouthful, her senses alive with the rich, earthy taste of Manipur. Vendors smiled as they watched her relish the flavours, nodding in approval. Thambal handed her a bamboo cup filled with lukewarm *laal cha*, a local tea, with an earthy aroma rising with the steam. She took a sip, savouring its subtle taste. The symphony of spices, textures, and aromas made her feel increasingly connected to Manipur with every bite.

As they continued, she found herself drawn not just to the food but to the warmth of the people who prepared it, with each dish carrying a story of heritage and tradition.

"This market is more than just business," Thambal said as they watched women barter and laugh. "It is where stories are shared, traditions are passed on, and identities are preserved."

She nodded, her eyes scanning the vibrant scene before her. The market was a living tapestry of history, each stall a testament to the resilience and strength of the women who ran it. She saw a mother instructing her toddler on how to sell fresh herbs while passing her a small cane woven basket. An elderly woman was telling stories to a customer in a rhythmic voice. The sounds of haggling and laughter created a backdrop, highlighting the ties that bound these women to their land and to one another. Thambal's words echoed in her mind—this market wasn't just about the goods exchanged; it was a space where culture, memories, and the soul of Manipur lived, breathed, and thrived.

A New Perspective

As the day ended, Gatha sat in De Avenue Cafe overlooking the bustling market. The sun dipped below the horizon, casting a warm glow over the streets of Imphal. From her seat by the window, she could see life unfolding in slow, meaningful moments—children laughing and elders engaging in conversations. The rhythm of Imphal felt comforting, like a song she had just started to understand.

For the first time, she felt a shift within her—a desire to learn more about this enchanting land and its people. The stories she had listened to, the places she had explored, and the people she had met were weaving themselves into something much bigger than just a travel experience; they were changing her.

Thambal joined her with a cup of black coffee and a warm smile. "So, what do you think of Manipur so far? Do you like this place?" he asked, placing the cup gently on the table.

"It's different," she admitted, her eyes gazing at a woman gently wrapping a shawl around her child outside the cafe. She paused to find the right words. "But in a good way. There is a depth here, a sense of belonging that I didn't expect. It's as if the land speaks through everything—the people, the flavours, the art, and even the silence."

Thambal smiled knowingly. "This is just the beginning. Wait until you see and experience the rest of it."

She nodded and took a sip of her coffee. The bitterness of the brew grounded her, balanced by the soft buzz of life outside the cafe. She leaned back, feeling a peace within her, as if she had finally started to listen to a part of herself that had long been quiet. As they planned the next phase of their journey, she felt a spark of enthusiasm and excitement.

Later that night, she returned to Hotel Imphal, the city lights dimming behind her as she stepped into the calm, softly lit lobby. The gentle hum of ceiling fans, the quiet shuffle of other travellers, and the soothing fragrance of lemongrass in the air welcomed her. In her room, she opened the balcony door, letting in the cool breeze. She placed her journal on the nightstand and sat for a moment on the bed, her body tired but her spirit awake.

As she rested her head against the pillow, she whispered to herself, "This place... It is different, and it is changing me."

And as the city outside gently slipped into sleep, so did she, with dreams filled not just with destinations and cuisines but with discoveries.

Manipur State Museum

The next day, early in the morning, Gatha enjoyed a hearty local breakfast of *puris* and *ooti*, a traditional, simple pea curry, before starting the second day of her tour. Thambal took her to the Manipur State Museum.

"Here, you will learn about the history, cultural diversity, and flora and fauna of Manipur," he said.

She was eager to dive deeper into the cultural and historical heritage of Manipur. Upon entering the museum, they were welcomed by a vast collection of artefacts, ranging from ancient Meitei manuscripts to tribal attire and traditional weaponry. The museum, located in the heart of Imphal, is one of the most important repositories of Manipur's heritage. It houses ethnological displays, archaeological discoveries, and natural history exhibits that reflect the intricate blend of the valley and hill cultures. One gallery showcased ancient coins and inscriptions, presenting a chronology of the region's dynastic history, while another was dedicated to royal regalia, featuring the traditional *pena*, a bowed musical instrument, and ceremonial outfits.

The museum's galleries highlighted the vibrant history of Manipur, showcasing its royal ancestry, the heroic stories of the Anglo-Manipur War, and the artistic skills of Manipuri dance and handloom weaving. A section allocated to the war displayed uniforms, weapons, and rare photographs from the era, providing insight into the valour and resistance of the Manipuri people.

As Gatha walked through the exhibits, she admired the intricate artistry of the ancient jewellery and pottery, marvelling at the elegant details of each piece. She was drawn by a captivating diorama of a typical Manipuri village, where miniature figures illustrated daily life. As they further explored the museum, she was enchanted by beautiful canvas paintings, each depicting vivid stories of Manipur's rich history and culture.

"These are so beautiful," she mused, observing the colours, brushstrokes, and emotions captured in the artwork.

"This is just a glimpse of Manipur's history and culture. As we travel, you will experience it even more vividly," Thambal said with a smile, watching her amazement grow with each discovery.

His words ignited a sense of excitement within her, making her eager to explore more. Every place she had visited so far deepened her understanding of Manipur's rich history and strengthened her appreciation for its living traditions. As they stepped out of the museum, the stories and images lingered in her mind, making her feel even more connected to the land and its heritage.

Andro Village – The Cradle of Pottery

After leaving the Manipur State Museum, still lost in thought about the exhibits, Gatha hardly noticed that the car had taken a quieter, greener route. The noise of the city faded into a gentle rustle of leaves accompanied by the distant melody of birds singing. As they drove past beautiful pine woods, rice fields shimmering in the late afternoon light, and scattered villages where children played barefoot on dusty paths, a sense of calm began to settle over her.

Thambal smiled at her, his eyes reflecting the warm golden light as they drove by paddy fields and small villages. "Now, we are going to a place that feels like stepping into the soul of Manipur—Andro Village."

Andro Village, a small town on the outskirts of Imphal, welcomed them with its traditional huts featuring *sumang* (the courtyard or space in front of a Manipuri house), adorned with a pot of water, some flowers, and a Tulsi *Chaura* (a place where Manipuri Vaishnavites worship the tulsi plant every day). The soft buzz of village life surrounded them. Nestled in the foothills of the Nongmaiching range, Andro is a living exhibition of Manipuri artistry, often referred to as the cradle of traditional pottery.

"Andro?" Gatha asked, the unfamiliar name rolling off her tongue slowly.

"Yes," Thambal nodded. "It is an old village famous for its traditional pottery and its remarkable ability to preserve ancient practices that have been handed down through the years. The small town of Andro also provides a fascinating glimpse into Manipur's wealth, offering everything from indigenous brews and traditional handcrafted goods to an ancient temple steeped in local legend." He paused before adding, "The people of Andro are dedicated to maintaining and conserving their slowly disappearing traditions. They are warm, welcoming, and skilled at producing a variety of handcrafted items."

She asked him curiously, "So, it is not just about the pottery?"

"No," he replied with a shake of his head. "That is one part of it, but it goes deeper. The villagers came together to create a cultural museum in 1993 under the direction of Mutua Bahadur, a renowned numismatist, writer, social worker, and anthropologist. Since then, it has served as the village's centre, where every practice and every handicraft holds its own memory."

"There is something resilient about this," she said softly. "To return, to reconstruct, and to move ahead with all that was once almost lost."

Thambal agreed, pride evident on his face. "That spirit is intricately intertwined into every aspect of life here. Our ancestors are known not just for their craftsmanship but also for their strong cultural identity. In a world that is constantly changing, they have managed to preserve their traditions."

Gatha was fascinated. "It sounds like a place where time stands still, where stories live in everyday activities. I feel like I am about to step into a live story."

"Exactly," he said with a smile. "This is about how you feel, not just what you see. Andro is a place where tradition is practised rather than merely preserved. It is more than just a village; it is our heartbeat. You'll see what I mean."

As they neared the village, she observed homes constructed from bamboo and thatch, integrating beautifully with the verdant landscape. The rhythm of life here was more relaxed, easy-going, and tranquil. Children ran barefoot down the unpaved streets, and the scent of burning wood and fermented bamboo shoots wafted through the air.

"The name 'Andro' is derived from the word *'handro'*. In the local language, it means 'the village of the people who returned'," he explained. "According to legend, the people of Andro were among the first inhabitants of Manipur. Forced to leave by a local ruler, they later returned to create their community and settle down. Eventually, they became known as The Andro."

Her eyes sparkled as they walked by a hand-painted sign that read, 'Welcome to Mutua Museum'.

"Have we arrived?" she asked.

He smiled. "Yes, and this is where history speaks."

The aroma of clay and wood smoke was carried in by a gentle breeze. They arrived at the Andro Pottery Museum, which fascinated her. It was not at all like a typical museum, usually located in a concrete building. Instead, the Mutua Museum, named after its first curator, is a collection of traditionally constructed thatched huts showcasing a variety of locally produced crafts. There were beautifully handcrafted earthenware pieces, each of them unique, moulded by the skillful hands of local women who had learned the art passed down through generations.

"This is the Mutua Museum," Thambal said, gesturing towards a bamboo hut. "It is named after its first collector and curator, Mutua Bahadur, who was born on January 20, 1948, at Imphal's Keishampath. This museum offers a whole new experience. Everything here is constructed as our ancestors did. No marble floors, no glass displays. Just the tradition, with fresh air in every nook."

There were different traditional huts representing the various communities of Manipur. The interiors of the huts were adorned with exquisitely made earthenware, each piece meticulously arranged. As Gatha strolled slowly along the rows, her fingers longed to feel the surfaces.

"They are so beautiful," she said admiringly. "Like each of these pieces has a soul and tells its own story."

"They do," he replied. "Every pot was made by the women in the village, using techniques passed down from mothers and grandmothers. It is not just a technique; it is a legacy."

Outside, they saw a woman seated on a small stool, moulding wet clay with practised elegance. Gatha watched carefully.

"She is not using a potter's wheel?" she asked, a surprised look on her face.

"No," Thambal replied. "That's what makes Andro's pottery special. They shape the clay with a flat wooden bat rather than a wheel. Look at how she is tapping it into shape. That's how they shape the pots."

She watched as the woman shaped the pot, her movements smooth and confident.

"What comes after that?" Gatha asked.

"The pot is allowed to dry in the sun for four days," he replied. "It is then fired and finally polished with a natural dye produced from the bark of the Corpus Dill Bata tree. That is what gives it that deep, earthy shine."

She smiled, keeping her gaze on the potter. "It is not just pottery—it is poetry in the clay."

He laughed. "You are absolutely correct. Pottery is not just an art; it is a legacy. The women are the keepers of the knowledge that is handed down through the generations."

Gatha knelt and picked up a pot, feeling the grooves made by fingers from ancient times.

"This feels like holding history," she said.

A few villagers nearby laughed and gently encouraged Gatha to try making a pot herself. Reluctant yet intrigued, she settled down and immersed her hands in the clay. As she began moulding the clay, her eyebrows knitted together in concentration. She laughed as she struggled to shape the clay into something even vaguely symmetrical.

"It looks easy when they do it," she said, "but this is so difficult to mould into a perfect shape. It takes so much effort."

Thambal laughed and replied, "This is not just about effort; it has a rhythm. It is something that takes time to develop."

Even though her pot was imperfect and wobbled on the mat, she smiled and said, "Well, this is soulful."

One of the women, named Ireima, spoke softly, "You are really talented, but according to our tradition, only married women in Andro are allowed to make pots."

"Really?" Gatha asked, surprised. "Why is that?"

"This is a customary practice," Ireima explained. "Before a woman begins practising pottery, she must be married. Furthermore, she cannot start until she has completed a ritual known as *'Thou Chanba'*, which translates to 'job assigning ceremony'. She is not considered ready to practise the craft until then."

With her hands still slightly soiled with clay, Gatha gazed down at her creation again.

"This sounds different," she said. "It is not just a technique; it is a ritual passage—a bond between generations."

Thambal agreed. "And every pot moulded here carries that legacy."

As they moved further, her eyes sparkled with curiosity.

"Check these out," she said, stopping next to a shelf filled with fragile tribal dolls. "They are dressed in various traditional outfits."

Thambal smiled, "These symbolize the twenty-nine tribes of Manipur. Each doll is handmade, highlighting the unique clothing and identity of each community. The dolls serve as a small homage to the state's diversity."

They continued exploring, looking at vibrant artworks, intricately carved wooden panels, and stone figures depicting ancient stories.

"More than just pottery, this place feels like strolling through a cultural tapestry," she said, facing him.

"That is exactly what it is," Thambal replied. "Each item here reflects people's memory—how they lived, what they believed, and how they viewed the outside world."

After finishing their tour of the museum's final exhibit, they left for their next destination in Andro. Thambal guided Gatha along a path that led to a peaceful temple. It was simple yet highly respected, with a thatched green roof, surrounded by a beautiful garden. At the entrance stood an ancient, inscribed stone.

"This is the 'Chakpa Panam Ningthou Meithoupirol Shanglen,'" Thambal said with deep respect. "Mei Mutaba', which translates to 'the eternal flame', is another name for it."

Her eyes traced the inscription on the stone at the entrance of the temple.

"It is beautiful," she said softly. "What is the story behind it?"

"This temple is dedicated to Panam Ningthou, the protective deity of Andro," he replied. "But what truly distinguishes it is the sacred fire that has been kept burning for almost a thousand years."

"A thousand years?" she echoed in disbelief. "That's amazing! How has it survived for so many years?

"With careful attention, tradition, and dedication," he answered. "According to legend, Poireiton, a mythical king of the Khuman clan, brought fire to Manipur in the first century AD."

"That is ancient history," she said, her eyebrows rising in awe.

He nodded. "It represented a crucial turning point for the people here. Prior to that, they lived as wandering hunters. However, under Poireiton's guidance and with the flame as a symbol, they began to establish themselves, creating agricultural communities. That fire became the beacon that illuminated the emergence of civilization in this area."

For a moment, they stood silently, feeling the weight of history surround them.

"So, this is not just about the fire," she said. "It is part of the heritage and identity."

"Yes," he nodded, his eyes fixed on the fire. "It is the soul of Andro, which is still burning."

They took blessings and started strolling through the village. Thambal pointed out a small group of huts with clay ovens and bamboo barrels outside.

"There is another tradition I want you to witness," he said. "Andro is not just known for its pottery; it is also famous for its native drinks."

She raised an eyebrow in curiosity. "Drinks?"

"Yes," he smiled. "Andro in particular. The villagers continue to make them the traditional way, employing techniques that have remained unchanged for hundreds of years."

"Andro is famous for two types of liquors, Wayoo and Machin. While Wayoo is a mild traditional beer, Machin is a kind of wine which has many medicinal properties."

He pointed to a man who was meticulously tending to a pot over a wood fire. "Did you see that? He is distilling Machin, which is produced by fermenting a mixture of local rice and the stems of a creeper plant called yangli."

"It smells sweet, like something to sip slowly on a rainy evening," she said, leaning in closer to inhale the warm, earthy aroma that filled the air.

"You are quite close," he smiled. "Machin has a soft, sweet scent, a malty taste, and a hint of smokiness. It is not just a beverage; it is integral to their rituals, celebrations, and even social gatherings."

She was captivated by the process. "So much care goes into it. It is not only about creating something; like everything else, it is about conservation."

"True", he replied. "Every step tells a story."

As they walked along the village roads, they were greeted kindly by many villagers, who offered them small bamboo cups of rice beer, a local delicacy, with warm smiles.

One of the villagers said to Gatha, "Please taste it."

After a moment of hesitation, she took the cup and savoured its earthy flavour.

"This is really refreshing!" she exclaimed, surprised.

Thambal nodded. "This is a drink you come to appreciate over time. The villagers take pride in it; this drink has been a part of their culture for many years."

Continuing on their journey, they set off for their next destination, Santhei Nature Park in Andro. As they drove, Thambal explained eco-tourism in Andro.

"Andro has recently started to embrace the concept of sustainable tourism," he continued as they got out of the car and began walking. "They are trying to promote eco-tourism in this region while being mindful of preserving their way of life and the land's natural beauty."

Gatha admired the natural beauty of the park. "This is the ideal location—untouched yet welcoming. They are finding a means to share their traditions without losing their uniqueness."

"That is the goal," Thambal said, smiling thoughtfully. "To let others in without altering Andro's essence."

He continued, "The villagers have constructed a lovely reservoir at the foot of the mountains and developed a park around it called Santhei Nature Park. They ensure it remains green and pristine, making it a popular spot for both visitors and locals."

Impressed, Gatha raised an eyebrow. "They seem to be putting in a lot of effort to maintain that balance."

"Yes, they are," he nodded. "Additionally, the number of tourists has increased with the establishment of an orchid farm near the park. It has been beneficial for the local economy, generating more job prospects for the villagers."

By the time they left Andro, the sky was painted in gentle shades of pink and orange, signalling the approach of evening. Gatha looked back at the village, admiring the view of the thatched roofs against the backdrop of the hills. The village's gentle rhythm lingered in her mind as a sense of calm enveloped her.

As they walked towards the vehicle, Thambal glanced at her with a smile. "Don't you think this is a unique kind of beauty?" he asked.

She replied, still immersed in her thoughts, "Yes. This place is more serene than the illustrious histories of kings or warriors. It is about the resilience of the people here, living harmoniously with their land, skills, and beliefs."

Before entering the car, Thambal took one last look at the village. "That is exactly what Andro is. It is not just about what you see; it is also about how you feel. The stories are not just in the temples or the pottery; they are in the people, the land, and the everyday moments."

With a gentle smile, Gatha faced him. "Andro has given me more than just views. It is a place that will stay with me, even after I leave," she said, pausing to look at the village one last time. "This place has gifted me stories to carry—tales expressed in smiles, shrines, and clay."

As Thambal drove back towards Imphal, she felt as though the village had become a part of her. Every moment seemed like a thread in a tapestry of eternity, from the aroma of fresh soil and the rhythm of the potter's hands to the sacred flame that had burned for centuries. Andro was not merely a place; it was a reminder of a deeper connection between people and their origins, a bond that transcends time. As the landscape faded into dusk, she realized she would always carry a piece of Andro with her—not just in memory but also in the understanding that some stories never truly disappear once they are shared.

Shree Shree Govindajee Temple

After leaving Andro Village, they made their way to Shree Shree Govindajee Temple.

"This is the main Vaishnavite temple of Manipur," Thambal said, his voice filled with respect and deep faith in God.

Gatha was awestruck as she gazed at the temple's huge entrance, featuring two gold-plated domes, a paved courtyard, and the white walls of the temple shimmering softly in the evening light. A beautifully kept garden extended alongside the temple, enhancing the peaceful ambience. In front of the temple stood a beautiful statue of 'Gai and Vasru'—a mother cow gently feeding her calf—a symbol of nurture and divinity. The temple's surroundings radiated tranquillity, with its simple yet beautiful design embodying the spiritual essence of Manipuri devotion.

They removed their shoes and stepped inside, their hearts filled with respect. The sacred atmosphere of the temple, accompanied by the subtle scent of incense lingering in the air, enveloped them. Gatha observed the high ceilings and polished floors that gleamed under the soft light of traditional oil lamps. The inner sanctum, or *garbhagriha*, housed the idols of Lord Jagannath—an incarnation of Lord Krishna—along with Balaram and Subhadra, all richly adorned in vibrant attire.

As they moved ahead, they realized they had arrived at the

perfect time—the *pujari* was about to begin the *aarti puja.* The rhythmic sound of bells and the soft chanting of prayers echoed throughout the hall, creating a divine and peaceful environment. Devotees gathered quietly, their palms joined and eyes closed in prayer. The flickering *aarti* flames danced in the dimly lit shrine, casting shadows on the walls. After the aarti, the pujari came forward and offered them *prasad* (food offered to God that is blessed and then distributed to devotees), which was sweet. Gatha received it with both hands, her right hand upside down, murmuring a silent prayer.

The warmth of the offering and the quiet grace of the moment left her feeling humbled and grateful, as though she had been gently touched by the divine. The pujari, a soft-spoken elderly man with kind eyes and a warm smile, noticed her thoughtful expression.

"Are you from Manipur, *beti*?" he asked in a gentle, curious voice tone.

She smiled and shook her head. "No, I'm visiting Manipur for the first time. This temple… it feels so peaceful, as if time stands still here."

He laughed softly. "That is the blessing of Lord Govindajee. His home welcomes everyone, no matter where they come from. This temple has been the spiritual heart of Manipur for generations."

She looked around, her eyes taking in the sacred space with renewed wonder. "It's beautiful. And there's something that feels so alive and positive here."

The pujari nodded. "This temple was originally built in 1846 during Maharaja Nara Singh's reign and was rebuilt by Maharaja Chandrakriti in 1876 after an earthquake. Even through wars and natural calamities, the people's devotion has never wavered.

Every morning and evening, we offer aarti. On festival days like Janmashtami, the temple overflows with song, dance, and devotion."

"I can feel it," she said softly. "Not just in the rituals, but in the smiles of the people. It's like God lives not just in the statue but in the hearts of the devotees."

The pujari smiled. "Yes, beti, you are right."

Before she turned to leave, she folded her hands once more and said, "Thank you."

He lifted his hand in blessing. "May Govindajee guide your journey and keep your heart open. There is much to explore in Manipur, but don't forget, true insight begins when the soul listens."

As she rejoined Thambal, Gatha turned back once again to view the temple, its white walls glowing softly under the evening sky. She held onto the pujari's words, feeling as though she had not only visited a sacred space but had also been gently reminded of the quiet, steady presence of something greater.

They sat there for some time, feeling peaceful and calm. There was a remarkable energy in the air—a positive energy that uplifted their souls and soothed their hearts. Gatha felt a divine presence, as if the walls whispered the ancient prayers.

As they exited the temple premises after the aarti, Gatha turned back for one last look. The temple, now softly lit under the early night sky, stood like a silent guardian of age-old devotion, its aura staying with her even as they walked away.

Back to Hotel Imphal

At night, she sat on the balcony, gazing at the starry sky, a view she rarely enjoyed in her bright, bustling city. Here, under the quiet veil of the Manipuri night, the stars twinkled like secrets waiting to be discovered. The distant chirping of crickets and the subtle fragrance of night jasmine drifting from a nearby garden enhanced her sense of calm. The serenity of it all enveloped her like a soft shawl, soothing yet awakening something deep within.

She felt a desire to explore and learn more about this place—its whispering stories and quiet secrets, the way the land breathed through its people, its traditions, and even its silences. She took out her journal and began to write, her pen flowing effortlessly across the pages, capturing the essence of her journey so far.

Kangla whispers the stories of kings and warriors, its sacred grounds still alive with echoes of the past. Ima Keithel is more than a market; it is Asia's largest market run by women. It embodies the spirit of Manipuri women, their strength woven into every trade and bargain. The Manipur State Museum felt like a time capsule, each artefact a silent guardian of a rich and resilient heritage. The chants at Shree Govindajee Temple made my heart still, and the prasad tasted like grace. And then came Andro—quiet, earthy, timeless. A village where clay becomes memory, moulded by the hands of women who carry generations of wisdom, where sacred fires have burned for a thousand years. With every step, I am not just learning about Manipur; I am feeling it, living it.

She paused, allowing her thoughts to settle. The paper fluttered slightly in the breeze, as if the night itself had read her words and agreed with them. She closed her journal for a moment, running her fingers over its worn cover, realizing this journey was more than just a visit. She looked up at the stars, a quiet smile playing on her lips. Perhaps, she thought, travel isn't always about going to new places; sometimes, it's about coming closer to yourself. With that thought nestled gently in her chest, she leaned back in her chair, letting the stars keep her company a little while longer.

****

II

A LAKE OF STORIES

Gatha's journey began early in the morning. The road to Loktak Lake was lined with rolling green hills, green rice fields, and quiet villages, each seemingly existing in a peaceful world. She stared out of the window, soaking in the scenery. She had heard of Loktak Lake, but the idea of a 'floating lake' still seemed abstract and otherworldly.

"Loktak is the lifeblood of Manipur," Thambal said, breaking the silence. "It is the largest freshwater lake in South Asia. The etymology of Loktak is derived from the Metei language, where 'lok' means 'stream' and 'tak' means 'the end'. It is not just a lake but a way of life for the people here. You'll see what I mean."

When they arrived at the lake, she was struck speechless. The vast expanse of water shimmered under the midday sun, dotted with patches of green that appeared to drift like tiny islands. The floating land masses, known as *phumdis*, were unlike anything she had ever seen.

"This is beautiful," she said, pulling out the camera from her bag.

He smiled, "It's not just beautiful; it also has stories to tell."

The Fisherman's Tale

Their first stop was a small wooden dock where Wangthoi, a local fisherman, waited with his narrow canoe. He greeted them with a warm smile and gestured for them to step in. He dipped his paddle into the calm waters, guiding the boat with skillful precision. As the boat moved smoothly across the water's surface, Wangthoi explained his life on the lake.

"I was born here, just like my ancestors," he said proudly. "We wake with the sunrise, cast our nets, and listen to the whispers of the water. My family has lived here for generations." With a calm and steady voice, he continued, "The floating islands you see are called phumdis. They are heterogeneous masses of vegetation, soil, and organic matter at various stages of decomposition, floating on the lake. The phumdis provide us with everything we need—fish, firewood, and even farmland." He then pointed to a small hut perched precariously on a phumdi. "That is my home," he said. "During the monsoons, the phumdis rise with the water. It feels like living in a floating world."

Gatha noticed the hut's thatched roof and bamboo walls, blending seamlessly with the floating vegetation beneath it. A fishing net hung outside, swaying gently in the breeze, and a small boat was secured close by. Life here was simple yet deeply connected to nature's rhythm. She wondered how Wangthoi and his family lived in harmony with the lake, their home shifting with the seasons, their survival tied to the movement of the water. She found it fascinating. She thought of how urban dwellers like herself took stability for granted, while people like Wangthoi adapted to the lake's ever-changing nature.

While roving the boat, Wangthoi said, "The lake is changing, though. Pollution, unregulated tourism, and the growth of water hyacinth are choking it. We are losing the phumdis, and with them, our way of life." He let out a heavy sigh, his gaze fixed on the shimmering waters that once teemed with life. "Our ancestors depended on this lake, not just for food but for identity and survival," he said, his voice full of sorrow. "But now, the fish are diminishing, the birds don't come like they used to, and the floating islands are breaking apart. If this continues, Loktak will be just another body of water—stripped of its soul, its people displaced, and its stories lost to time." The weight of his words hung in the air as they approached the centre of the lake, where the phumdis were the largest and most stable. The beauty of Loktak was undeniable, but so was its fragility.

The National Park: The Only Floating National Park

Thambal then guided Gatha to Keibul Lamjao National Park, located on the southern edge of the lake. It is the only floating national park in the world and is home to the endangered Sangai deer, a subspecies of Eld's deer found only in Manipur. As they stepped onto the spongy phumdi-covered ground, Gatha felt a strange sensation beneath her feet—solid yet slightly yielding, as if the earth itself was alive. She felt spongy but firm, an intricate layer of vegetation, decomposed organic matter, and soil floating on the water's surface.

Thambal gestured toward the tall grasses swaying in the breeze. She scanned the landscape, her heart quickening at the possibility of spotting the brow-antlered deer, which was difficult to find. The stillness of the park was mesmerizing, broken only by the rustling of reeds and the distant call of water birds. After a quiet trek, they spotted a sangai grazing in the distance. Its trim silhouette, elegantly curved antlers, and graceful movements appeared almost otherworldly.

"The sangai is more than just an animal to us," Thambal explained in a hushed tone. "It is a symbol of our identity. We call it the 'dancing deer' because of the way it moves gracefully across the floating land."

She watched in quiet anticipation as the golden light of the late afternoon cast long shadows over the landscape.

"The sangai's steps are delicate yet deliberate," he continued, his voice filled with profound respect. "It knows the land beneath it shifts, so it moves as if in rhythm with the lake itself."

Just then, a rustling caught their attention. Gatha held her breath as another sangai emerged from the reeds, its slender legs stepping cautiously onto the floating ground. It paused, ears twitching, before continuing forward. In that moment, she understood this deer was not just a creature in the wild; it was a living connection between the people and their land, an enduring emblem of Manipur's soul.

"But if the lake dies, so does the sangai," Thambal added.

She felt the weight of his words, realizing that saving this fragile ecosystem meant preserving not just nature but an entire way of life. She stood there for some time, watching in awe, feeling an inexplicable connection to this land.

Sendra Island: A View from Above

In the evening, Thambal took Gatha to Sendra Island, a hillock offering panoramic views of Loktak Lake. The climb was steep, but the view from the top was worth every step. From the peak, she observed the lake stretch endlessly, its surface shimmering in the fading sunlight. The phumdis resembled green spots on an enormous silver canvas. Tiny boats scattered across the water, and wisps of smoke curled up from the dwellings on the floating islands.

"This is where I come when I need to think," he said, sitting on a step. "Loktak is not just a lake. It is alive. It breathes, nurtures, and sustains. But it is also fragile, and we must protect it."

Gatha nodded, her thoughts racing. The lake was not

just a natural wonder; it was a storybook of human resilience, environmental balance, and cultural heritage.

A Conversation with the Lake

As night fell, they returned to Wangthoi's hut on a phumdi, where the stillness of the lake seemed to deepen. Gatha sat on the edge, her feet dangling above the water, while Thambal prepared their local tea, known as laal cha, on a small stove. The aroma of the brewing laal cha wafted through the air, carrying hints of smokiness and spice that blended perfectly with the crisp breeze from the lake. As she took the warm cup, the steam curled around her face, and she felt a sense of calm settle over her.

The world seemed to slow down here, each sip connecting her a little more to this enchanting place. The gentle sway of the phumdi beneath them and the distant calls of birds created a moment of serenity. She could not help but think that perhaps this was what she had been searching for—an unspoken connection to the world beyond the noise and chaos of her everyday life. She thought about the interconnected lives she had glimpsed—Wangthoi's struggles, the endangered Sangai, and the harmony of the floating islands. Each was a thread in a piece of cloth that was both beautiful and fragile.

"I feel like the lake is speaking to me," she said softly.

Thambal smiled and replied, "It is. If you listen closely, it tells us its stories."

She sipped the tea, feeling a newfound sense of purpose. The lake was more than just water and floating islands; it was alive, holding within its depths the memories of generations. And now, it was sharing its secrets with her. She had come to Manipur as a journalist, but Loktak Lake had transformed her into a storyteller.

A Night Under the Stars

At night, as Gatha sat by the side of Loktak Lake, watching the phumdis drift lazily on the water, she reflected on everything she had experienced so far. Manipur, with its mix of history, culture, and natural beauty, had opened her eyes in ways she had never expected. The resilience of the people, the quiet strength of their traditions, and their ability to adapt to the changing world were both humbling and inspiring. The stillness of the lake mirrored the calm that had settled in her heart.

She had arrived in Manipur uncertain, unsure of what to expect from a place so far from the world she knew. But as she looked out over the water, she felt a deep sense of belonging—not to the land itself but to the spirit of the place. The journey had allowed her to explore not only the heart of Manipur but also the depths of herself.

Thambal joined her on the shore. "You have seen so much of Manipur, Gatha. But there is still more to experience," he said, his eyes reflecting the stars above. She smiled. "This journey has been more than just about exploring new places."

She opened her journal and began writing about her beautiful, unique experience:

> *Loktak is not just a lake—it is memory in motion. The lake whispers many stories quietly. Today, I experienced the floating islands, guided by Wangthoi, whose life is as fluid and as rooted as the phumdis. His tale was about fishing, inheritance, identity, and survival.*
>
> *I also saw the rare sangai deer that walked like poetry across the phumdis. The land here speaks—in wind and in silence. At Keibul Lamjao, the ground beneath me felt alive with each step. At Sendra, the lake looked like a living map of*

stories – green islands floating on shimmering water. I didn't expect to find stillness here. I came here as a journalist seeking stories and the whispers of the land, but I found something deeper—belonging.

The wind carried the peaceful sound of rippling water, a reminder that the journey was far from over. There were more stories to uncover, and she was ready to continue her exploration, to uncover the layers of Manipur that still lay hidden.

****

III
THE LEGACY OF MOIRANG

As Gatha and Thambal were leaving Moirang, the atmosphere was filled with a mix of nostalgia and calm determination. Their next destination in the town was the Moirang INA Memorial, a place that serves as a testament to the courage of the Indian National Army (INA) during the Second World War. It stands tall as a tribute to those who once dreamed of an independent India. The INA, under the leadership of Subhas Chandra Bose, fought alongside the Japanese army to oust the British from India. The Moirang Liberation of 1944 was a significant event, marking the first time the INA raised the Indian flag on Indian soil.

The bronze figure of Netaji Subhas Chandra Bose, with his arm raised in resistance and optimism, seemed to watch over them as they stood in solemn reflection. His eyes, though cast in metal, appeared alive with conviction; he was a leader inspiring his people to always remember the price of freedom.

"During the war, Moirang was a symbol of resistance," Thambal explained as they walked through the memorial, which housed relics from the era, including photos, weapons, handwritten letters, INA uniforms, and weathered documents that bore witness to a turbulent time. "It was here that the Indian flag was first hoisted on Indian soil in 1944—an event that continues to be celebrated by Manipuris as a moment of pride in our fight for independence."

Inside the memorial, the museum area was peaceful and respectful. The walls were covered with news clippings from around the world, maps of wartime operations, and portraits of INA troops. Gatha's attention was drawn to a worn-out picture of Netaji speaking to the INA soldiers. His message, inscribed on a glass panel below, read, "Give me blood, and I shall give you freedom." The power of that declaration struck her deeply, more than ever before. She stood before the memorial, her thoughts swirling under the weight of history. She had studied the freedom struggle in school, but witnessing the tangible proof of that battle, so deeply rooted in the soil of Manipur, gave her a new perspective on the sacrifices made by the people of Manipur in India's freedom struggle. The memorial, in that moment, was no longer just a historical site; it was a living, breathing chapter of a story still echoing in the hearts of the people. She ran her fingers over the engraved names of the brave soldiers, her eyes lingering on the words that spoke of sacrifice and valour.

"They fought with nothing but courage," she murmured.

Thambal nodded, feeling the weight of history pressing upon him. "And they proved that freedom is never given; it is taken."

They stood there quietly, the wind softly stirring the surrounding trees, as if nature itself were honouring those who had sacrificed their lives. A group of schoolchildren arrived, their conversations subdued as they approached the memorial, their eyes widening at the statue of Bose and the powerful exhibits within. Gatha's heart filled with hope as she observed them in silence. These stories will never be forgotten, she thought. They will live on in the hearts of the next generation.

As they began to depart, she took one final look at the memorial, illuminated in the soft glow of the evening sun. It stood not only as a tribute to the past but also as a symbol for the future—a reminder that the spirit of sacrifice and resistance continues to reside in the land of Moirang.

Voices of Resilience

Next, Thambal introduced her to Leima, an elderly woman who had lived through the struggles and challenges of the INA and witnessed firsthand the impact of the Japanese occupation in Manipur. Leima lived in a simple house on the outskirts of Moirang.

"Life was never the same after the war," Leima recalled, her voice filled with both sorrow and strength. "We had lost many of our young men, and the occupation brought so much suffering. But we did not give up. We kept going because we believed in something greater than ourselves."

Leima's words resonated with Gatha. It was easy to study history and perceive it as a distant event. But being face-to-face with someone who had endured it made the challenges and struggles of the past come alive in a very real way. The people of Manipur had faced numerous challenges, but they had also demonstrated remarkable strength.

Leima showed them a worn-out black-and-white photograph of her brother, who participated in the INA War and never returned. She touched the photo frame gently, her fingers tracing his face.

"He died for a dream," she murmured, "a dream we still hold close."

In that quiet, humble home, Gatha felt the weight of sacrifices made by ordinary people for the extraordinary cause of freedom. It was not just about battles or leaders; it was about families, about strength in the face of fear, and about holding on when everything else was lost. She realized then that Manipur's history was not just confined to museums or memorials; it lived on in the hearts of its people, in stories like Leima's, passed on like treasures of dignity.

As they said their goodbyes, Leima pressed Gatha's hand and said, "You must carry our stories with you, child. Let everyone know we were here, and we endured."

Gatha nodded, silently promising to become a keeper of those voices. After sitting in the car, she opened her journal. With no words to express her emotions, she just wrote a few lines:

> *"History is not a page in any textbook; it is a heartbeat in the soil. Leima's eyes carried decades of untold pain and strength. She reminded me that freedom is earned, preserved, and remembered—every single day. It was a proud moment to witness the place where the first flag of free India was raised. Manipur doesn't just remember its past—it breathes it."*

She learned that the freedom struggle was not just a historical event for the Manipuri people; it was a living memory, passed down through generations, a thread that wove the community together.

****

IV

MYSTERIES IN THE HILLS

The morning air was refreshingly cool as Gatha and Thambal drove away from the shimmering stretch of Loktak Lake, their destination now the distant hills that rose like green giants on the horizon. The serene beauty of the lake had left a lasting impression on Gatha, but the thought of exploring the mysterious hills to the north intrigued her even more. The hills of Ukhrul, a place rich in folklore and steeped in quiet majesty, awaited her.

As they left the plains behind and began climbing the hills, the roads became narrower and steeper, winding through thick forests and highland meadows.

"This is where the land speaks," Thambal said, his voice filled with deep respect. "The hills of Manipur are not just geographical features; they carry stories as old as time itself, hidden in the mist and shadows of the mountains."

She wasn't sure what he meant, but she was eager to find out. The attraction of the unknown tugged at her, and as they drove deeper into the hills, she felt the air grow denser, heavy with mystery. She had read about Ukhrul before coming here, but no book could capture the sheer beauty and mystique of this place.

They arrived in Ukhrul by evening, exhausted from the long journey. Their accommodation for the night was at the 25-Degree North Hotel, nestled amidst the serene hills. After settling in, they took a moment to appreciate the cool breeze and the quiet charm of the town. With an early departure scheduled for the next morning, they chose to get some rest, conscious that the journey ahead would be equally exciting and adventurous.

The Phangrei Mountain

Their first stop was Phangrei Mountain. The mountain, according to local legend, was the home of Phungreitang, the spirit that watched over the entire region. Towering above the lush valleys, its slopes were covered in a dense blanket of wild flowers. The villagers believed that Phungreitang's presence could be felt in the cool mountain breeze and the rustling leaves, as if the spirit whispered secrets of the land to those who were willing to listen.

As they climbed higher, the air became sharper, and the distant echo of a bird's call seemed almost like a greeting. The journey was difficult, with steep climbs and dense forest paths, but Gatha's excitement grew with each step. The higher they climbed, the more magical the surroundings seemed. Mist rolled in from the distant peaks, covering the path in a mystical glow. The air was thick with the scent of pine and damp earth.

"Phangrei is more than just a mountain," Thambal explained as they walked. "It is a living being. Every rock, every tree has its place in the story of this land. Our ancestors believed that if you treated the mountain with respect, it would guide you."

She felt a coldness in the atmosphere. The respect for the mountain was evident, and with each step, she could feel the weight of its mysteries. At the peak, the view was breathtaking. Beneath them, Ukhrul looked like a tiny hamlet tucked away among the hills. The valleys stretched infinitely, and the peaks of faraway mountains towered like silent guardians. The silence was profound, as if the mountain itself was holding its breath.

Thambal pointed to a lake there and said, "Phangrei Lake is

a small hilltop lake that is a popular picnic spot for locals. People camp here by the lakeside to observe the stars in a clear night sky."

They stayed a little longer, allowing the moment to imprint itself in their memory. Gatha stepped closer, her eyes scanning the lake, feeling a direct connection to the past. A respect took root in her—for the land, its mysteries, and the silent wisdom carried by the hills.

The Legendary Shirui Hills

They continued their journey towards Shirui Kashong, as Phangrei Mountain seamlessly connected with the rolling expanse of the Shirui Hills. This area is home to the world-famous Shirui Lily (*Lilium mackliniae*), a flower that blooms only in these hills of Manipur—found nowhere else in the world. It is regarded as one of the natural wonders of Manipur. The flower is a light shade of pink, and its bell-like petals create a bowed shape, resembling an act of worship towards a supreme deity. What is distinctive about this flower is that it displays seven colours when viewed under a microscope, which cannot be perceived by the naked eye. The Shirui Lily was declared the state flower of Manipur on March 21, 1988.

These scenic hills rise to an elevation of approximately 1,730 metres (5,675 feet) above sea level, offering breathtaking views of lush greenery, rolling landscapes, and peaks covered with fog. The Shirui Lily, named by the British botanist Frank Kingdon-Ward, who discovered it in 1946, blooms only between May and June each year. With its delicate pink and purple shades, the flower is revered by the locals, particularly the Tangkhul Naga community, who consider it sacred.

As they climbed the gentle slopes, a cool breeze carried the faint scent of wild flowers, mingling with the freshness of the mountain air. The path was lined with lush greenery, and the distant chirping of birds filled the silence.

Thambal pointed to a patch of land covered in buds yet to open, their delicate petals waiting for the right moment to bloom. "This flower is believed to be a gift from the spirit of the hills. Our ancestors say that the spirit, known as Shirui Kashong, protects this land," he explained. "Every year, Manipur celebrates the Shirui Lily Festival, showcasing the cultural heritage of the Tangkhul community through folk dances, music, and local crafts, while also promoting conservation efforts for this delicate flower."

Gatha bent down to observe the delicate petals. She had read about the rare flower, but now, standing here, she felt the sacred energy that surrounded it. The soft pink and purple hues seemed to glow under the morning sun, their fragile beauty untouched by time. A gentle breeze rustled through the leaves, as if whispering secrets of the land's ancient past. The locals believed the Shirui Lily was more than just a flower; it was a guardian of the hills, a symbol of resilience and grace. In that moment, Gatha understood why.

A visit to Shirui Hills was not just a journey into nature but also a step into the heart of Manipur's rich traditions and ecological treasures.

The Return to the Village

As the day wore on, Gatha and Thambal headed back to Ukhrul. The sun began to set behind the hills, casting long shadows over the village. The air had become chilly, and the lights from the houses twinkled like stars in the darkening sky.

Thambal then led Gatha to a traditional Tangkhul village. The Tangkhul tribe, one of the oldest in the area, has resided in these mountains for centuries. Upon arrival, they were welcomed by Shanngam, a respected elder of the community. He usually didn't speak much, but his presence exuded wisdom and strength, his wrinkled face telling the tale of a lifetime spent in the hills.

"Welcome to our land," he said as they entered his home, a traditional wooden house with thatched roofs, surrounded by terraced fields. "Here, the land is not just what you walk on; it is alive and holds stories."

Shanngam's words seemed to echo the essence of the land itself. While they sat on woven mats, enjoying a meal of rice and bamboo shoot curry, he began to share stories passed down through generations.

"Our people believe the hills are home to spirits," he began.

"While some spirits may not be kind, they are integral to our existence. The rocks, the trees, and even the rivers—all possess spirits."

Gatha listened intently, fascinated by the deep connection between the Tangkhul people and their land. The hills were more than a mere habitat for them; they were sacred, and the very soil beneath their feet was a living, breathing entity.

That night, after finishing their meal, they built a bonfire outside and gathered with a few villagers, the warm blaze projecting twinkling shadows around them. As they sat around the fire with the Tangkhul villagers, Gatha reflected on what she had learned. The hills represented more than merely a physical landscape; they served as vibrant vessels of tales, myths, and ancestral knowledge. The people who lived here understood the land not just as a place to inhabit but as a companion in their existence, a spirit to be honoured and respected.

Thambal looked at her with a knowing smile. "The hills are full of stories, Gatha. Some are told, and some remain hidden."

She nodded, feeling a deep sense of gratitude. The mysteries of the hills weren't just about myths or legends; they were about understanding the relationship between the people and the land, a bond that transcended time and space.

As the flames popped, she pulled out her notebook and began to write, capturing the spirit of the Tangkhul tribe's connection with the hills:

> *"The hills of Ukhrul are not just beautiful; they are alive. Phangrei whispered ancient secrets in the wind, and Shirui revealed a sacred bloom found only in this soil. Every step I took felt like walking across a page of a story older than time. Shanngam's stories reflected the truths woven into the forests. Here, people honour and celebrate nature. Tomorrow I will be moving, but a part of me will always stay behind—listening for the next whisper…"*

She realized that the mystery of a place was as much about the stories we share as it was about the tales we choose to withhold.

****

V

THE SACRED CAVES

Early next morning, they enjoyed a hearty local breakfast of Tan (a traditional Manipuri flatbread that looks like a puri) and Aloo Kangmet (a simple yet flavourful dish of mashed potatoes with mustard oil, chillies, garlic scapes, and ngari) served with laal cha. The delectable breakfast gave them energy for the journey ahead. As they packed their belongings and stepped out into the chilly morning air, the fog-covered hills seemed to beckon them.

"We will be exploring the holy caves of Manipur today," Thambal said. "Manipur's hills and forests conceal caves that are not just natural structures but living chapters of history, spirituality, and mythology. Many of them are associated with ancient legends, tribal traditions, and even resistance movements."

As they drove through winding mountain roads, Gatha was filled with excited anticipation. The landscape changed with each turn, revealing thick woodlands, flowing waterfalls, and glimpses of villages where time appeared to have its own rhythm. Their destination, Khangkhui Caves, promised an encounter with Manipur's mystical past.

Khangkhui Cave

Khangkhui Cave, also known as Khangkhui Mangsor Cave, is well-known for its natural limestone formations. Situated in Manipur,

India, the cave holds notable historical and archaeological significance, with traces of ancient human habitation discovered within its chambers.

"This cave is not just a natural wonder but also a testament to our rich history," Thambal said proudly. "According to legend, a king named Mangsorwung constructed chambers within the cave for his wives and sons. In certain versions of the tale, the king is referred to as the Devil King. The largest hall in the cave functioned as the throne room for the king. The cave contains a pit known as *Shirata,* meaning falling star hole, in the regional Tangkhul dialect."

"This place is incredible," Gatha said, her voice filled with wonder, while taking out the camera to capture the beauty of the place.

The cool air carried a subtle sound of water falling, enhancing the cave's mysterious presence. She glided her fingers over the moist texture of the stone, sensing the weight of history beneath her fingertips. Detailed rock patterns, naturally sculpted columns, and delicate mineral deposits shimmered under the torchlight. What made the cave even more intriguing were the limestone formations hanging from the ceiling and those rising from the ground, creating a surreal experience.

"The ancestors of the Tangkhul people believed that the cave was home to a protective deity," Thambal said. "Excavations conducted by archaeologists have revealed that the cave served as a habitat during the Stone Age. The cave has yielded Palaeolithic artefacts, such as combs, kettles, and plates," he continued.

"It feels like stepping into another era. Imagine the people who sought shelter here—what secrets and stories these walls could tell," Gatha said, running her fingers over the rough rock formations. She turned to Thambal, excitement shining in her eyes. "It seems like entering a realm where nature and history unite in breathtaking harmony."

"The cave also served as a refuge for local inhabitants during World War II when the Japanese troops moved into Manipur and the neighbouring Nagaland," Thambal added.

A sense of both wonder and respect filled the air as they stood there, surrounded by centuries of unspoken tales.

Mova Cave

Their next destination was the Mova Cave, also referred to as the Hundung Mova Cave, located near Hungpung village. Mova Cave is one of the most captivating tourist attractions, offering a glimpse into the enchanting world of nature's artistry. This hidden gem is renowned for its stunning limestone formations and fascinating geological features, making it a favourite spot for adventure seekers and nature enthusiasts alike. As Thambal and Gatha moved towards the cave, the verdant hills and pleasant surroundings created a perfect landscape for exploration, offering a sense of peace that is difficult to find in busy urban environments.

Thambal introduced Gatha to the guide.

"This is Sana," he said, gesturing toward the man standing beside him.

Gatha greeted him with a polite smile, observing his calm demeanour and the trace of curiosity in his gaze. Sana nodded in acknowledgement, his eyes briefly examining Gatha before he began to speak.

"Welcome," he said in a warm yet measured tone. "I hope you're ready for the journey ahead."

Gatha felt a quiet sense of anticipation stir within her—this was the beginning of something unknown, and she was eager to see where it would lead. Sana guided them through the cave and to the nearby waterfall, explaining every detail along the way.

"Visitors to Mova Cave enjoy the serene surroundings, including the crystal-clear water of the Lungshang River that flows nearby. This is the main chamber of the cave," he said, stopping.

"It is spacious," Gatha said in awe.

"Indeed, it is large enough to accommodate more than 100 people at the same time," Sana replied.

The moist air carried the faint fragrance of moss, and the noise of water droplets falling enhanced the cave's tranquil ambience. Stalactites hung like icy blades from the roof, forming an enchanting view inside the cave.

"According to legend," Sana continued, "Mova Cave is considered a sacred female entity, and the steep rock mountain nearby is believed to be her male counterpart. The locals say they were once celestial lovers who were separated and turned to stone, forever yearning for each other."

Gatha felt a shiver run down her spine as she listened to the story, her imagination weaving the tale with the ancient rocks surrounding her. For a moment, it felt as if the cave itself was alive, guarding the love story within its depths.

"The entire cave is divided into four zones," Sana explained. "The first zone is the entrance of the cave; the second zone comprises the main hall; the third zone consists of a narrow passage where visitors must kneel to get through; and the last zone leads to the exit point by the river."

Gatha was fascinated by the deep connection between nature and folklore. As she took in the breathtaking scenery, she couldn't help but appreciate how the cave wasn't just a natural marvel but also a sacred place filled with stories and mysteries passed down through generations. The soft whisper of the river outside added to an enchanting ambience. She traced her fingers across the cool, damp walls, imagining the countless travellers who had walked this path before her, each carrying their hopes, fears, and respect for the cave's ancient spirit.

"This place offers tourists nature walks and an opportunity to immerse themselves in the peaceful and relaxing beauty of Manipur's countryside," Thambal said. "The combination of natural beauty and cultural narratives makes Mova Cave a truly special destination," he added.

Exploring the cave was a thrilling experience for Gatha. As she navigated its twisting corridors, she came across distinctive rock formations that seemed to whisper tales of nature's evolution, shaped by time, water, and the elements. The interplay of light and shadow within the cave created an almost dream-like setting, enhancing its mystical charm. She paused to listen to the rhythmic flow of the river, feeling as if the cave was alive, holding mysteries within its depths.

They returned to the village, wrapping up their day's adventure. Although Gatha felt a deep sense of peace, sleep eluded her as her mind replayed everything she had experienced and learned about the caves—their history, their legends, and how nature had sculpted them over time. Unable to calm her thoughts, she pulled out her journal and thoughtfully wrote:

> *"Whether you are a photography lover eager to capture breathtaking landscapes, an explorer looking for a new adventure, or a traveller seeking peace in nature, Mova Cave will undoubtedly leave a lasting impression on your journey through Manipur."*

As she closed her journal, she sensed the presence of the cave still lingering within her. The memory of the moist earth, the fragrance of wild flowers, and the soothing whisper of the river filled her senses once more, deepening her connection to the sacred place she had just discovered.

Tharon Cave

The next day, they embarked on a journey from Ukhrul to Tharon Cave, nestled deep in the heart of Tamenglong. They were eager to uncover yet another hidden marvel of Manipur while carrying with them the cherished memories of Khangkhui and Mova caves. The journey took seven to eight hours, with their route twisting through mist-shrouded hills, dense forests, and winding rivers, each turn unveiling the untamed beauty of Manipur's landscape. As they progressed, the refreshing mountain air heightened Gatha's excitement about what awaited her at their next stop.

"Tharon Cave, also known as Thaeuluan Cave, is 655.6 metres long, with five exits and 34 junctions," Thambal explained, his voice echoing. "Approximately 12 caves can be found beneath. Tharon Cave is recognized for its historical significance and intricate formations. It is an adventure filled with mystery and exploration."

Gatha was amazed. Her eyes widened as she gazed at the large stone outside the cave, where a detailed map had been engraved and painted for tourists. She stepped closer, tracing her fingers lightly over the markings, trying to grasp the layout of the cave before them.

"This map helps visitors navigate every corner and turn inside the cave," Thambal said, gesturing at the various routes carved into the rock. "It also guides them through the alleyways. This cave is believed to be magical, with various chambers such as the Lovers' Hall, the Dancing Hall, the Meeting Hall, and others hidden within its depths," he continued.

She listened intently, absorbing every detail he shared. The thought of huge, hidden chambers filled her with wonder and curiosity. What mysteries did those ancient chambers hold? As she stood at the entrance, a cool wind from inside brushed against her face, as if inviting her to step in and unravel the secrets that had been preserved over centuries.

"Believed to be over a thousand years old, Tharon Cave is said to be home to fruit bats and features complex chambers and narrow passages," he continued, his tone rich with wonder. "The cave's maze-like structure, consisting of five interconnected tunnels, has long intrigued explorers and historians alike. Archaeological excavations have revealed evidence of the Hoabinhian culture, an ancient civilization that once flourished in the region. The cave holds secrets yet to be uncovered."

Gatha's imagination ran wild with thoughts of the past. She could almost picture ancient tribes seeking shelter within these very walls, their voices lost to time, but their presence still lingering. The air inside carried a musty odour, and faint echoes of dripping water resonated through the tunnels, adding to the cave's mystical allure. As they entered the cave's dark, mysterious depths, the air grew cooler, and the walls seemed to whisper stories of a forgotten past. The dim glow of their flashlights flickered across the uneven rock formations, uncovering detailed patterns sculpted by the passage of time.

The further they explored, the more the cave seemed alive, its corridors winding and twisting like a maze of mysteries. As they moved through the narrow tunnels, they came across an open room—the renowned Dancing Hall. The floor was smooth, almost as if it had been carved by ancient hands. Legends spoke of spirits that had once danced here. Gatha felt a chill at the thought, a mix of fear and thrill coursing through her.

Each step into the cave felt like a journey through history, where every turn could reveal a hidden chamber or a relic left behind by those who had once inhabited this place. The caves stood like guardians of forgotten wisdom, quietly waiting for those willing to listen to their whispers.

A Night in Tamenglong

As evening descended and the last rays of sunlight faded beyond the rugged hills, Thambal and Gatha emerged from Tharon Cave, their minds still buzzing with excitement and amazement. The refreshing mountain breeze welcomed them as they walked out, their bodies fatigued from the long exploration. The day had been filled with adventure, but now exhaustion was settling in.

"We should stay the night in Tamenglong," Thambal suggested, glancing at the sky painted in hues of orange and deep purple.

Gatha nodded in agreement, eager to rest and reflect on the mysteries they had uncovered. They made their way to a BG Hotel nestled amidst the rolling hills, which offered a peaceful ambience. As they settled in, the aroma of a locally prepared meal filled the air—steaming rice, smoked meat, and fresh bamboo shoots. Over dinner, they spoke in hushed tones, recalling the strange silence of the cave, the soothing sound of rivers and waterfalls, and the ancient halls.

"It's incredible how much history lies hidden beneath our feet," Gatha mused, stirring her tea.

After a hearty dinner, she kept thinking about her experience and the mysteries and stories of the caves. She held her journal close, knowing the pages would soon be filled with everything the day had left behind. She then opened her journal and began writing about her experience:

"Today, I walked through silence carved in stone. Each place

felt alive, not just with the breath of nature but with whispers of folklore and memories. The walls of these caves didn't just hold up the earth; they held stories. They are the quietest storytellers of history. There was a moment in Tharon Cave when all sound faded, and I could hear my own heartbeat echoing. In that moment, I felt a strange connection with all those who had walked this path before – from the Stone Age settlers to modern seekers like me. I will never forget the feeling of having stepped into the womb of time, where something whispered. I guess a part of me will always remain within the cool, shadowed stillness of these sacred caves, where history breathes in every drop of water and chiselled stone. Here, nature doesn't just surround you—it speaks to you, if one is willing to listen."

Later that evening, as they rested beneath the star-filled sky, the distant noises of the jungle soothed them into peaceful sleep. The mysteries of the caves still lingered in Gatha's mind, but at that moment, she welcomed the tranquillity of Tamenglong, knowing that another adventure awaited her with the rising sun.

****

VI
THE HIDDEN GEMS

Gatha's journey through Manipur was far from over. There was so much more to explore.

"I would recommend exploring the less-travelled areas, each offering its own distinct narratives, cultures, and scenery," Thambal suggested. "These destinations hold the true essence of Manipur's diversity and are frequently missed by visitors," he added.

She agreed enthusiastically, her anticipation rising at the thought of venturing beyond known paths. Together, they planned their travels for the upcoming days, ensuring they would uncover Manipur's hidden gems, its legends, and its rich history by visiting these places sequentially.

Their itinerary included visits to secluded spots, exploring hidden natural wonders, and tasting rare delicacies prepared using traditional methods. Gatha knew this part of the journey would be different—more engaging and personal. She was no longer just a traveller; she was a pursuer of stories, a learner of culture, and a witness to the soul of Manipur. The path ahead was unknown, but that was what made it all the more thrilling and exciting. With Thambal guiding her and the promise of new discoveries ahead, she stepped into the next chapter of her adventurous journey, ready to embrace all that Manipur had yet to reveal.

The Barak River – The Natural Marvel

As they were in Tamenglong, they started their journey from the Barak River, one of Manipur's natural marvels—a true hidden paradise surrounded by abundant greenery.

"The Barak River is Manipur's largest river," Thambal said. "Tipaimukh Dam, a multipurpose hydroelectric dam, is proposed on this river," he continued.

"This is beautiful," she said, gazing at the mesmerizing sight of the Barak Waterfalls.

As they stood near the tumbling waters, the misty spray from the waterfall refreshed their faces, creating a delightful moment. The rhythm of the flowing water merged beautifully with the chirping of birds and the swaying of leaves in the surrounding forest. Gatha took a deep breath, inhaling the fresh, earthy scent of the wilderness.

"This place feels untouched, like nature's hidden treasure," she said, watching the rays of the sun dance on the glistening water droplets.

Thambal nodded. "Only a few people visit here, but those who do never forget its beauty."

They enjoyed their time, soaking in the tranquillity and listening to the soothing sound of the Barak River. Gatha felt a rare connection to nature.

They stopped at a small hotel for lunch, where he introduced her to *Kangsoi*, a simple traditional water-based stew or curry that is completely oil-free. It is prepared by cooking vegetables and herbs in boiling water flavoured with dried fermented fish (ngari).

"This is so soothing and tasty," she said, savouring every bite.

He smiled and offered her some more warm broth of kangsoi.

After lunch, they left for their next destination. The midday sun cast golden tones over the landscape as their vehicle navigated through rolling hills and dense forests. Gatha watched the changing scenery with each passing mile, wondering what awaited them ahead.

Jiribam – The Gateway to Manipur

By the time they reached their destination, Jiribam, night had begun to settle over the town. Jiribam, a small yet significant town on the westernmost edge of Manipur, bordering Assam, served as a gateway to the state.

"Jiribam is known for its natural beauty, greenery, and scenic landscapes," said Thambal.

Gatha, soaking in the beauty of this place, smiled peacefully. It was a place that whispered tales of tranquillity and peace. Fatigued from the journey but eager to explore, they headed to the renowned Jiribam Bazar, a lively market filled with the sounds of merchants and the fragrance of fresh goods. Stalls overflowed with vibrant fabrics, beautiful bamboo items, and aromatic spices, showcasing Jiribam's cultural diversity. The air buzzed with the calls of vendors selling their goods while buyers negotiated prices with skillful finesse. Among the crowd, they noticed an elderly woman weaving a traditional shawl.

"Look at these beautiful traditional shawls, Gatha!" Thambal exclaimed, pointing to the elderly woman's stall.

Gatha ran her fingers across the delicate threads, admiring the artistry. The woman's hands moved with skilled elegance as she wove the shawl.

"How long does it take to weave one shawl?" Gatha asked, watching in fascination.

The woman looked up with a warm smile. "It depends on the design," she said. "It can take a few days, or sometimes weeks."

Gatha decided to buy one as a souvenir, thinking that the

market was not just a place of trade—it was a living testament to Jiribam's cultural vibrancy. Many locals, primarily from the Bishnupriya Manipuri community, proudly shared their cultural heritage, a beautiful blend of Manipuri and Bengali traditions.

"You should try this!" said Thambal, buying a small leaf-wrapped package from a vendor.

She opened it to discover freshly prepared *pitha*, a traditional rice cake. "This tastes delicious!" she exclaimed, taking another bite.

They then visited a local eatery, where she tried *chamthong*, also known as *kangsoi*, and *chakhao amubi* ('chakhao' means delicious rice, and 'amubi' means black), the black rice of Manipur. The flavours of the food reflected the simplicity of Jiribam.

"This is amazing," she said, savouring the delicious flavours of the dish. "It feels so comforting."

Thambal agreed, replying, "That is the beauty of Manipuri cuisine. Simple, yet deeply connected to nature and tradition."

"Jiribam plays a crucial role as a trade gateway, connecting Manipur to the rest of the country," he continued. "Goods from the valley and the hills travel through Jiribam, making it a central hub of commerce and cultural exchange."

After finishing their dinner, they headed to a small guesthouse close to the Jiri River, whose waters glimmered in the moonlight.

That night, while Gatha rested in her guesthouse, she realized that each place she explored was a piece of Manipur's vast and diverse tapestry. With the Jiri River's soothing rhythm echoing in her mind, she drifted into peaceful sleep, looking forward to the next chapter of her journey.

Churachandpur – The Resilient Crossroads

At dawn, after enjoying a hearty local breakfast, they headed southwest, travelling along twisted roads and scenic views, with the shifting colours of the sky marking the passage of time. By evening, they finally arrived in Churachandpur.

"This is the second-largest and one of the busiest cities in Manipur," Thambal said, glancing at the bustling streets.

Gatha nodded while observing that the town was alive with energy—shops lit up the streets, street vendors served hot, steaming delicacies, and the air buzzed with conversations in various dialects. Churachandpur's vibrant tribal markets were treasure chests filled with handcrafted shawls, baskets, and bead jewellery. While wandering through the market, Thambal introduced her to an artisan weaving a beautiful shawl.

"These are handmade by local artisans," he said with pride. "Each design is unique in its own way."

"They are beautiful," she said, admiring the intricate embroidery.

"This is *puandum* ('dum' means black, and 'puan' means cloth), a traditional shawl symbolizing honour and status among the locals," the artisan explained with a welcoming smile.

She could not resist buying one as a souvenir.

Thambal smiled and said, "Good choice, Gatha."

They found a seat near a food stall, the warmth of the place adding to the quaint charm of the town. There, they ate dinner, savouring the flavours of the region. The smoky aroma of *vawksa rep* (smoked pork with mustard greens and garlic added to boiling water) and the comforting warmth of steamed black rice filled their senses.

With the day's journey and exploration behind them, they checked into the peaceful Geiljang Resort, located on the slope of a verdant hill with views of the foggy Churchandpur hills and lake. The resort combined contemporary amenities with traditional aesthetics, featuring wooden cottages with sloping roofs, spacious balconies with small swing chairs, and panoramic windows that overlooked picturesque lakes and hills. A soothing natural symphony created by the cool evening breeze surrounded them.

Inside Gatha's cottage, warm golden lighting gave the space a cosy glow. As her mind wandered back to the day's marvels, she settled into the soft bed, the quilted blankets wrapping her in warmth. Feeling emotionally fulfilled and physically exhausted, she recognized that this was the perfect spot to stop, reflect, and prepare for the next phase of her adventure.

The next morning, feeling refreshed and eager to explore, they set off towards one of the town's highlights—the Zogam Tribal Museum in Tuiboung.

"This museum preserves the history and traditions of the tribal communities," Thambal explained as they entered.

Her eyes widened as she took in the collection of artefacts—ancient tools, finely crafted textiles, and traditional jewellery that spoke of a rich cultural past. Her fingers glided along the rim of a handcrafted bamboo basket.

An elderly curator welcomed them with a smile. "These artefacts narrate the journey of our ancestors—how they lived and what they valued," he said. "Each tribe has its own unique heritage, but together, they form the soul of this land."

She listened intently as he explained the significance of the elaborate headgear, war drums, handwoven cane and bamboo baskets, bead jewellery, and ceremonial shawls on display.

"It's incredible how tradition and culture are preserved despite changes over time," she remarked.

The curator agreed. "Our history is our identity. That is why we ensure the younger generations never forget it."

After immersing themselves in history for a while, they departed for the picturesque Khuga Dam, where the calm waters reflected the surrounding hills, creating a stunning view.

"This place is incredible!" she exclaimed, as the wind ruffled her hair.

Thambal nodded and said, "Khuga Dam is not just a tourist attraction; it serves a multipurpose initiative. It is primarily for irrigation and drinking water, but it also represents progress in Churachandpur. This dam, constructed across the Khuga River, holds back the river to form a reservoir. Inaugurated in 2010, the dam also generates hydropower." After a brief pause, he added, "This is a popular spot where visitors come to appreciate nature and the scenery. It is a peaceful getaway for tourists and a relaxing picnic spot for locals."

The water surface sparkled like scattered diamonds as the golden rays of the sun illuminated it. The surrounding hills stood in peaceful silence, their lush green slopes gently rolling towards the horizon. The breeze that rustled through the thick grass carried with it the smell of the earth.

They saw a group of boys skipping stones as they walked along the waterside. A boy yelled, "One, two... three, go!" as his stone glided smoothly over the surface of the water.

"That's the finest one so far, Thonglen!" another friend applauded with a smile.

Gatha looked over the shimmering water. "There is something magnificent about places like this... where nature and human efforts unite."

Thambal looked at the rolling hills and said, "Everything is connected—the past, the present, the people, and the land."

She smiled, "I don't understand how a dam can retain so much history. This is just lovely."

"Perhaps that is why these places are important," he replied. "They remind us we are part of something larger that we didn't create on our own."

The faint chirping of birds, the cool breeze, and the tranquil ambience provided a perfect place to unwind before they moved on to Ngaloi Waterfall. At the waterfall, she stood at the brink, admiring the sparkling water.

"This place feels so peaceful, a real hidden treasure," she said, closing her eyes and taking a deep breath.

He nodded. "It's a favourite spot for locals, still unexplored by many tourists," he said with a sigh. "The dam not only supplies water but also adds to Churachandpur's beauty," he added after a brief pause. The falling water, tumbling over rugged cliffs into a crystal-clear pool below, was a mesmerizing sight. They took a moment to appreciate the beauty and tranquillity of nature before heading to their next destination.

Their final stop of the day was the mysterious Tonglon Cave, steeped in history and folklore. Near the cave was the serene Tonglon Waterfall, which had a mystical charm. The rhythmic sound of falling water resonated through the nearby cliffs as they approached, beautifully blending with the sound of trees gently rustling in the wind. Golden rays of sunlight danced on the surface of the crystal-clear pool at the base of the waterfall, which tumbled elegantly over weathered stones. Gatha paused for a moment, captivated by the view.

Bending down to touch the cool water, she said, "This feels like something lost in an old book."

Smiling next to her, Thambal said, "The locals think these waterfalls possess a spirit that is mysterious, just like the Tonglon Cave."

"Is that true?" she asked. "The place seems ancient."

He nodded. "Yes, it is ancient. Many people believe that this entire region is holy. Long-distance travellers would gather here to relax."

Leaving the tranquil waterfall behind, they headed towards the cave. Gatha admired the ancient rock formations, sculpted over centuries, and imagined the stories hidden within the walls as they navigated through the cave.

"This cave is one of the best cultural and historical highlights of Churachandpur," Thambal stated with pride in his eyes. "The writings and carvings found in this cave have helped historians understand Manipur's past more clearly."

Gatha listened intently while diving deeper into this hidden treasure. As they progressed further into the cave, the faint light created haunting shadows, and the atmosphere felt heavy with the passage of time.

"It's both thrilling and frightening at the same time," she said.

He agreed. "That's the beauty of such places that still remain unexplored by many to date."

She felt a strange connection, so she opened her journal and wrote:

"History is not just a story we read or study about; it is something that we can step into."

She closed her journal, feeling a deeper admiration for Churchandpur's rich cultural and natural heritage, making it a memorable day to remember.

Exhausted from the day's journey through remarkable places, they made their way to a cosy local eatery for their evening meal. The enticing aroma of sizzling dishes and freshly prepared local delicacies filled the air, immediately stimulating their hunger.

They ate smoked pork, paired with a spicy bamboo shoot chutney and a bowl of steamed rice. The warmth of the meal provided a sense of comfort after the long day. After dinner, they returned to the resort, their fatigued bodies embracing the assurance of a peaceful night ahead of the upcoming journey.

Chandel – A Tribal Wonderland

Early in the morning, they began their journey further south. The refreshing breeze brought a fresh, earthy fragrance. As they navigated through twisting roads, the fog gradually dissipated to uncover lush green hills. By midday, they arrived in Chandel, a district known for its cultural diversity.

"This place feels incredibly pristine," Gatha said, gazing at the rolling hills.

"It certainly is," Thambal replied. "There are only a handful of visitors who have discovered this gem. Chandel is inhabited by numerous indigenous tribes—Anal, Maring, Lamkang, and others. Each tribe possesses its unique customs, languages, and traditions."

As they walked through a small village, they were warmly welcomed by locals dressed in colourful traditional attire. Men wore loincloths, similar to *dhotis*, while women donned sarongs, paired with beautifully handwoven, embroidered shawls and headgear.

An older woman smiled at them. "Welcome to our homeland," she said in a soft, gentle voice.

"Thank you," Gatha replied.

They followed her to explore the village. The villagers were hosting a small tribal community feast. They joined them and learned about their tribal customs and traditions. After the feast, Gatha participated in a traditional fire ritual, a holy ceremony symbolizing harmony between humans and nature. The elegant movements of the dancers, paired with rhythmic drumbeats, created a mesmerizing scene.

"This dance is part of our harvest festival," the old woman explained. "We celebrate Mother Earth, our ancestors, and the blessings and gifts we receive."

Gatha watched in admiration. "It's remarkable how deeply traditions are intertwined with everyday life here."

Later in the afternoon, they explored the village, observing daily life unfold—women crafting textiles on traditional looms, children playing around thatched-roofed homes, and elders imparting wisdom beneath the shade of large banyan trees. This experience left Gatha with a deep appreciation for Chandel's vibrant cultural heritage.

As the sun began to set, painting the sky in shades of orange and purple, she realized how much she had learned in just a few hours. The kindness of the people and the richness of their traditions made this journey one of the most rewarding experiences of her travels. She fell asleep peacefully, thinking of the next place she would visit.

Tengnoupal – Gateway to Serenity

The next day, they embarked on their journey to Tengnoupal Pass, the highest point on the Imphal-Moreh road, which was stunningly beautiful. From the pass, Gatha could see the vast plains of Myanmar stretching into the horizon.

"This view is unreal," she said, leaning slightly out of the car window to take it all in.

Thambal smiled and said, "It's one of the most picturesque routes in Manipur."

The refreshing mountain breeze carried the earthy scent as

they stood atop Tengnoupal Pass, taking in the breathtaking panoramic view. The distant plains of Myanmar merged seamlessly with the rolling hills of Manipur, creating a beautiful contrast of landscapes. Gatha was amazed by this historical pass, which was once a crucial trade route. They stopped at a viewpoint, soaking in the stunning natural beauty. She stretched her legs and took out her camera to capture these beautiful landscapes.

"Do you want to taste that?" Thambal asked, pointing towards a tea stall.

They approached the stall, where the vendor handed them steaming cups of black tea infused with local herbs.

She took a sip, feeling the warmth. "This is so refreshing and earthy."

As they stood there, she sighed, "Every place we explore seems magical."

He smiled, "That's what travel does to a person. It reminds us how vast and beautiful the world is."

His words resonated with her. As the sun began to dip behind the hills, they visited the famed Laxmi Hotel located on India-Myanmar Friendship Road. Sitting cross-legged on woven mats, they savoured local delicacies like *champhut* ('cham' means simple, and phut means boil), a simple vegetarian dish made with vegetables like mustard leaves, shoots, carrots, cabbage, peas, bottle gourd, and cucumber, boiled without spices or strong flavours. They also enjoyed *zawlaidi,* also known as the 'Love Potion', a grape wine that paired perfectly with the meal. The kindness of their hosts and the rich cultural experience left Gatha with a profound respect and appreciation for the heritage of Tengnoupal.

With contented hearts and fulfilled appetites, they retired for the night, the echoes of tribal songs and the flickering firelight marking the end of another unforgettable day.

Thoubal – A Blend of Natural Beauty and Rich Culture

Another day began with a journey to the core of Manipur: Thoubal, a hidden treasure renowned for its natural beauty and cultural richness. Surrounded by rivers and farmlands, Thoubal is a paradise for those seeking peace.

Thambal took Gatha to Kakching Garden, a picturesque landscaped area located at the foot of the Kakching Hills. The peaceful surroundings, filled with blooming flowers and lush green lawns, provided an ideal setting for reflection on her journey.

"One of the most cherished places in Thoubal is Kakching Garden, also known as Kakching Leikol or the People's Garden," he explained as they walked along the winding stone path. "It is located south of the Kakching Bazaar on Uyok Ching Hill. People come here to escape the hustle and bustle of everyday life. It is peaceful here... almost divine."

Gatha admired the flowerbeds bursting with colour and the walkways lined with well-trimmed bushes.

"It is so soothing," she said. "This place looks like a beautiful painting."

Thambal nodded in agreement. "This carefully designed garden provides a serene retreat. Visitors can enjoy tranquil water features, well-kept lawns, and colourful flowerbeds that display a mix of native and exotic plants."

"I understand why this place is so popular," she said, smiling as a family passed by with a picnic basket. "It seems like the kind of place one would visit to unwind and recharge."

"True," he replied. "This place is popular with families, couples, and solo visitors seeking a rejuvenating and aesthetically pleasing environment. The well-maintained paths and seating arrangements enhance the total experience, making it an ideal place to relax and enjoy the natural beauty of Manipur."

Gatha took a deep breath, enjoying the floral fragrances wafting by. "This place is both welcoming and lovely. It feels as if it invites you to unwind and linger for a bit."

"That is exactly the idea," Thambal replied with a smile. "It's not just a beautiful spot; here you will find sacred shrines such as Ibudhou Pakhang Laiseng and the Mahadev Temple, along with a statue of Hao Sampubi, a legendary guardian from our mythology. There is also a small restaurant, a beautiful park, and stunning city views surrounded by hills. According to the locals, you haven't truly experienced Kakching until you have spent some time here."

As they walked further into the garden, she stopped next to a fanciful topiary that resembled a green elephant. Laughing, she said, "The plants have personality, too."

"This is our green elephant," he chuckled along with her. "Children adore it. We believe the garden should feel vibrant, not simply look attractive."

They continued to wander together. The nearby hills stood tall and quiet, as if they were ancient guardians watching over the park. Gatha felt a surge of emotion in her heart.

"I have experienced so many things in Manipur," she said after a moment of reflection. "Not only the traditions and celebrations, I have also witnessed how deeply people are connected to their land and to one another."

He nodded. "Yes. Manipur focuses not just on its attractions but also on its soul. And once you feel it, it stays with you forever."

They made their way to a restaurant hidden among the trees.

Thambi placed an order, "One *chasubi* and *bora* (*pakoda* from Kakching, which is only available here)."

Curious, Gatha asked, "Chasubi? What is that?"

He smiled and replied, "Consider it our take on a spicy

pizza. However, you won't find it anywhere else; it is exclusive to Kakching. It's crispy, tasty, and full of local spices and ingredients."

She eagerly took her first bite. "This is amazing! Why isn't it known worldwide?"

"Maybe it's better that way. Some things are best kept local. It increases their value," he smiled.

Then, he took her to the Khongjom War Memorial, the site where Manipuri soldiers made their last stand against the British in 1891. The Anglo-Manipur War, which occurred in Khongjom, Thoubal district, is commemorated at the Khongjom War Memorial Complex.

"This is the best place for history lovers," Thambal said, with a smile on his face.

They stood in front of a 30-foot-tall entrance, an arch-like structure with three pillars, each symbolizing a martyr. At the top of the entrance, swords were placed in the middle.

"This is where our forefathers fought bravely, even knowing they were outnumbered," Thambal continued, his voice filled with pride.

As they moved further, they walked through tranquil lakes, lush valleys, and magnificent hills, offering a sensorial experience.

"This place is so peaceful and full of natural beauty. The view pleases the eyes and soothes my soul," Gatha said.

He nodded with a smile. They soon reached the world's tallest sword statue.

She looked at it in awe. "I have read about this in a book, but standing here… it feels truly different. It's as if this place is whispering history," she said.

"They say the wind here carries their whispers," he replied. "They fought not just for our kingdom but for our identity. This

32-foot-tall sword statue symbolizes the courage and sacrifices of Manipuri warriors. They are the pride of Manipur. The statue stands for the courage, dedication, and patriotism shown by the freedom fighters of Manipur, who defended against the British Army's simultaneous attacks from three fronts: Kohima, Silchar, and Myanmar on April 23, 1891."

She asked, "Who was their leader?"

"Major Paona Brajabashi," he replied. "He is one of the most respected heroes. The British promised to spare his life when he was captured if he betrayed his nation. But he chose to die rather than live in disgrace. The most important battle of the Anglo-Manipur War was the Battle of Khongjom."

She turned to him, her eyes shining, "Do people still remember their sacrifice?"

"Yes, on April 23rd every year, we celebrate Khongjam Day, commemorating the martyrs of the Anglo-Manipur War," he replied. "This memorial also includes a museum that displays various artefacts and documents related to the battle."

They looked around the Khongjam War Memorial Sankirtan Hall and then sat near a pond with crystal-clear water in the centre, enjoying the greenery from the grass fields and the pleasant atmosphere. Gatha felt at peace, taking in the panoramic view of the memorial.

Then they left for Waithou Pat, a picturesque spot surrounded by paddy fields and fruit orchards. It appeared lovely with the midday sunlight reflecting off the water's surface.

"Waithou Pat is an oval-shaped lake," Thambal stated. "The Ningthibi canal serves as the water source for Waithou Lake."

"This place is stunning," she said, gazing at the glistening water. "It seems as though time slows down here."

Thambi laughed. "That's the magic of Thoubal. This lake is

renowned for its picturesque landscape, but were you aware that this place previously had plentiful fish like Ngaton and other species?"

"Really?" she asked, with curiosity on her face.

"Yes, but over the years, things have changed. A number of fish species just died," he said with a sigh. "Still, local families visit this place to relax and enjoy the scenery, capture the moments on camera, and savour tasty pineapples. On certain mornings, you might even observe fog emerging from the water. It feels like heaven."

She was sitting by the lakeshore, her feet swinging in the dream-like water, enjoying the pristine natural beauty of the lake.

"It seems as though nature is whispering its secrets to me," she said.

"Look at that boat over there," Thambal said, pointing to a small canoe moving smoothly across the lake, where a fisherman was skillfully casting his net. "Fishing is a way of life in Manipur."

She breathed in deeply. "This place is beautiful, peaceful, and relaxing. I understand why it holds such significance."

He smiled, "Still, you haven't tasted the pineapples here. Come on, let's eat some."

They went to a small fruit stall where an elderly woman was cutting fresh pineapples, adding a pinch of red chilli powder and a pinch of salt. She offered them a plate, smiling kindly.

Gatha took a bite, her eyes lighting up. "These pineapples are amazing! They are the best I've ever eaten. The sweetness and the spice—it's just perfect!"

Thambal laughed. "I told you. The pineapples here are the best you will ever have. Once you try these, you won't want to eat pineapples from anywhere else."

She nodded, unable to resist the sweet, juicy, freshly cut pineapples.

As they savoured the fruit, the golden light of the sunset sparkled on the lake, enveloping the moment in a warm, unforgettable glow. The serene beauty of the lake, combined with the warmth and hospitality of the locals, created an experience she would treasure forever.

On their way back to Imphal, they stopped at a cosy place called Coffee Culture in Waithou. The fragrance of freshly brewed coffee welcomed them as they found a comfortable seat.

"This place is perfect," Gatha said, holding a warm coffee mug.

Thambal smiled, stirring sugar into his coffee. "This is one of those places that quietly surprises you—simple, but just right."

She looked at the fading light. "I feel like I have stepped into a postcard."

"That is the thing about Manipur," he replied. "It hides its beauty. You just have to slow down enough to notice."

They sat in pleasant silence for a moment, sipping their coffee.

"I think this is the kind of memory that stays with you," she said softly.

He nodded. "True."

She closed her eyes, her heart full of quiet gratitude for the stories, the food, the land, and the people who had welcomed her like family.

As night descended, they enjoyed a hearty dinner, savouring the delightful tastes of local dishes. With their bodies tired from the day's explorations but their hearts brimming with happiness, they retired for the night. Gatha fell asleep, dreaming of the beautiful place and its cultural richness, looking forward to the journey that lay ahead.

Kangpokpi – The Vibrant Hill Town

Their next destination was Kangpokpi, a lively town known for its pristine villages and stunning mountain treks. The town was also famous for its warm hospitality.

"Are you ready for the trek?" Thambi asked.

Gatha eagerly responded, excited to stretch her muscles. "Yes, let's go! I am ready for it!"

"Ok. We will be hiking to the highest peak in Manipur, Mount Koubru. This place is well-known for trekking, camping, and nature exploration. Many adventurers and pilgrims trek to the peak to enjoy the picturesque beauty and experience the spiritual energy and peace," he said with pride in his eyes.

She smiled in excitement. "I have been looking forward to this adventure for a long time."

He smiled back. "We are good to go then. Just make sure to pace yourself. The view from Mount Koubru is worth every step."

As they began to walk, a refreshing breeze sifted through the trees. Gatha took a deep breath, feeling the crisp mountain air fill her lungs.

"This place already feels magical—a true hidden gem," she said, looking around in wonder.

Thambal nodded, "This region is rich in biodiversity, with a variety of flora and fauna. It is a habitat for various species of animals and birds, making it an important ecological zone."

With excitement building at every step, they continued their journey up the rugged path, ready to embrace the adventure ahead. After hours of hiking through dense woods and rugged paths, they finally reached the peak of Mount Koubru. The sight that welcomed them was breathtaking—vast rolling hills, lush green valleys, and a sky painted with shades of orange and purple as the sun began to set.

Gatha stood mesmerized, her heart filled with a profound sense of tranquillity and achievement. "This is so beautiful," she murmured, her eyes exploring the horizon.

Thambal smiled, gazing at the beautiful scenery, "Yes. This place is very important to the people of Manipur. It is not just about the view; it is about the spirit of the mountain. They say that Lord Koubru, the guardian deity, watches over this land from here."

After the lengthy journey, they arrived back at the village, where the residents of Kangpokpi hosted a feast, a grand gathering where laughter and music filled the air. Long wooden tables were lined with hot dishes of smoked meat, bamboo shoot curry, and freshly prepared rice. The food looked tempting, and Gatha felt hungry immediately.

A woman wearing a traditional shawl offered her a plate. "We invite you to join us. You are our guest, and here, guests are treated like family."

Gatha smiled warmly, "Thank you. Everything here smells incredible."

She took a bite, and her eyes widened, "This is delicious! The flavours are so rich. Everything is simple yet perfectly balanced—just perfect."

The kindness of the people, the laughter, and the flavours created a sense of home for her, as if she had always belonged there. Both Thambal and Gatha sat by the crackling bonfire alongside the villagers, listening to folk songs and tales that had been passed down through generations. The rhythmic sounds of traditional drums resonated in the night air, merging with the laughter and conversation of the gathering.

After some time, a woman offered Gatha a cup of warm herbal tea. "Please, have a drink," she said with a kind smile.

Gatha took a sip and felt the warmth spread through her. She glanced around at the shining faces of the villagers, the flickering firelight dancing in their eyes. At that moment, she realized this night, this place, would remain with her for eternity.

Under the vast, star-filled sky, she sensed a deep connection with the land and its people. As the weariness from the day's travels settled in, she thanked her kind hosts and went to bed. She slipped into a peaceful sleep, dreaming of the adventures and marvels that lay ahead.

Senapati – The Land of Heritage and Nature

Gatha's last destination on the tour was the gently sloping hills and vibrant greenery of Senapati, a stark contrast to the busy city of Imphal. It is known for its rich tribal heritage. Thambal took her to Mao village, a picturesque place.

"Filled with culture and blessed with peace, Mao is a lovely hill town located in the Senapati district of Manipur state," he said proudly. "It is home to the renowned Mao tribe from Nagaland, along with several other local communities."

Gatha listened intently and nodded. As they approached Mao village, she took a deep breath, allowing the fresh air to fill her lungs. She was struck by the beauty of the cherry blossoms lining the path leading to the Mao Gate. They were breathtaking.

"This seems surreal. It looks like a painting. This is so lovely," she said, her eyes wide with wonder.

Thambal stopped the car to allow her to appreciate the scenery fully.

"You are very lucky to be here during the blooming season," he said, pointing to the delicate pink blossoms gently swaying in the wind. "Every year, we celebrate the Cherry Blossom Festival here. The entire village comes to life with dance, music, and traditional cuisine."

Her eyes sparkled in fascination, "That sounds enchanting. I have always heard about cherry blossoms in Japan, but I was unaware that Manipur had them as well."

He laughed softly. "Indeed, and we are very proud of that. The Mao people have a strong connection with nature. These flowers are not just beautiful; they symbolize renewal and hope."

Gatha inhaled deeply, relishing the experience, "It feels like I am not just seeing a place, but experiencing a part of a story."

Thambal smiled. "That's precisely what Mao village is—a living story waiting to be told."

After a few hours, they travelled further towards the Mao Gate.

"This is Mao Gate," he said, gesturing toward the grand archway. "It marks the border between Manipur and Nagaland."

Gatha stared at the archway, its architecture rising prominently against the scenic hills. The atmosphere felt different, as if she were standing at the junction of two realms.

"So, is Nagaland just beyond this?" she asked, her voice filled with amazement.

He nodded. "Yes. Every day, numerous travellers pass through this gate. It is not just a border but a gateway connecting cultures, traditions, and histories."

As they stood there, a soft breeze stirred among the trees, carrying whispers of countless journeys through Mao Gate over the years.

As the golden shades of the setting sun painted the sky, they began their journey back to the village. The evening breeze was refreshing, carrying the subtle fragrance of soil and flowers. As they walked, Gatha breathed in satisfaction. "Today's journey was amazing—no words can express it. From the cherry blossoms to Mao Gate, I felt as if I had entered a new world filled with untold stories."

Thambal smiled. "I told you, the more you explore, the more you will be surprised to learn about new places and their untold stories and mysteries. That's the magic of Manipur."

As night fell over Mao village, Gatha realized this place had left a mark on her soul. It was beyond just a place to visit; it was an untold story she would carry with her forever.

Early next morning, Thambal led her to a small local market where craftsmen exhibited their handmade goods, baskets, and jewellery. She appreciated their talent and creativity.. During their visit, she learned about the Poumai Naga culture, their customary clothing adorned with detailed beadwork, and their historical stories.

After exploring the market, Thambal took her to Willong Khullen village. When they arrived there, her eyes widened at the view in front of her. Towering stone monoliths over 10 feet high and a few over one metre wide, a total of approximately 135 pillars, stood tall against the sky, their surfaces worn by the passage of time.

Gatha ran her fingers over one of the stones, feeling its rough, ancient surface. "This is unbelievable," she said. "It looks similar to Stonehenge, but I have never heard that such a place exists in India, and that too in Manipur."

"Yes, only a handful of people are aware that a small village in Manipur, a rarely visited Northeastern state, is home to such a marvel, the same as Stonehenge," he said. "This remarkably captivating monument is, unfortunately, not appreciated by many locals of Manipur, except for those who stay near Willong. These monoliths have remained here for centuries, and no one truly knows how they were placed here. Some think they were raised up by our ancestors," he concluded.

Gatha looked around in wonder. "So, they hold stories that got lost in time."

He smiled. "That's right. The elders claim that these stones communicate with one another at night, and each stone has its own name."

She felt a slight shiver, not from fear but from the eerie beauty of the narrative. As they stood in the presence of the towering monoliths, a soft breeze swept through the trees, as if the stones were sharing their untold stories with the evening air.

As night fell, they sat by a cosy, flickering fire, along with elders who shared ancient tales in the village. The rhythmic rise and fall of their voices painted vibrant pictures of warriors, spirits, and lost legends. The air was filled with the aroma of local delicacies. Gatha enthusiastically tasted a fragrant Manipuri rice dish mixed with bamboo shoots pickle and herbs, then enjoyed a hearty porridge made with rice, vegetables, and smoked meat. The simplicity of the flavours carried an earthy richness that reflected the deep connection between the people and their land.

Taking another bite, Gatha turned to the villagers, "This is extremely tasty. The flavours are so unique and soothing."

Just then, an elderly woman laughed, pointing to a small basket filled with fiery red chillies. "Have you ever heard about our Naga King Chili or Umorok Chili?" she asked.

Gatha looked at the chillies with curiosity, "I have read that it is one of the hottest chillies in the world!"

The elderly woman agreed, her eyes sparkling. "True, just a tiny bite can burn your mouth! But for us, it is a treasured ingredient. It enhances the taste and adds flavour to our food."

"Would you like to try some?" Thambal asked, laughing.

Gatha hesitated for a moment, then took a small piece. As soon as she put the chilli on her tongue, a fiery sensation coursed through her mouth. She started breathing heavily, waving her hand in front of her face. "That's... spicy!"

The villagers burst into laughter, and a woman offered her a cup of steaming herbal tea, "Drink this. It will help to reduce the burning sensation."

As Gatha drank the tea, the warmth of the fire, the joyous sounds of the villagers, and the echoes of ancient stories enveloped her like a gentle hug. That night, as she lay in bed, she sensed a change within her—a profound, unspoken connection with the land, its people, and its untold stories.

A Journey of Wholeness

Gatha's journey through Manipur had led her to places she had never imagined, introduced her to flavours she had never tasted, and plunged her into cultures that profoundly motivated her. Each area she explored possessed its unique allure, weaving together a rich tapestry of traditions, resilience, and beauty that defined Manipur.

Returning to Imphal, she chose to spend a few more days immersing herself in the rhythms of traditional music, enjoying Manipur's diverse cuisine, and experiencing the vibrancy of its festivals. The city, with its blend of history and modernity, seemed familiar yet filled with new discoveries to her.

That night, as she made herself comfortable in her room, she thought about the journey that had transformed her in unexpected ways. She took out her journal, her fingers gliding over the worn pages, and began to write:

Manipur is not just a place; it is an emotion, a poem that stays with you for a long time, whether it is the misty hills, dams, waterfalls, caves, rivers, and monoliths of Manipur or the culture, heritage, warmth, and hospitality of its people. I arrived as a traveller, but I will leave as someone who carries a piece of Manipur inside them forever. I will not just carry the memories; I will carry the spirit of this land that has whispered its stories into my soul.

I will always remember the surreal sight of cherry blossoms, symbolizing renewal and hope. I will never forget the sacred silence of Koubru, the highest peak, where the first light paints the sky in hues only nature can create. The tallest sword statue that whispered unspoken secrets. I will remember the sacred caves that whispered ancient stories and the museums that spoke of deep-rooted history in valour and tradition. How could I ever let go of the feeling of standing beneath a cascading waterfall, its waters washing away not just fatigue but every worry, leaving behind a sense of renewal; the vibrant crossroads, where there is a beautiful tapestry of shared heritage and harmony; and the Manipur-Myanmar border, where history, trade, and traditions continue to weave a story of unity in diversity?

I will always remember the rhythmic beats of drums echoing through the villages, the flickering flames of bonfires where the tales of ancestors were told, and the warmth of strangers who welcomed me like family. I will cherish the flavours of every dish I tasted throughout my journey and the laughter shared over cups of laal cha. Each sunrise over the hills and every sunset by the lakeside felt like nature's own masterpiece, reminding me of the timeless beauty this land holds.

For me, Manipur is not just a journey; it is a transformation. It is not just seen; it is felt—in the gentle touch of woven fabrics, the soulful melodies of tribal songs, and the unspoken bond between its people and their land. I have walked its sacred paths, gazed in wonder at its monolithic structures and the cherry blossoms, and danced to the rhythm of its festivals. With every step, I have learned, evolved, and connected in ways I never imagined.

With a satisfied sigh, Gatha closed her journal, knowing that the essence of this journey would stay with her forever. Yet, a part of her wasn't ready to leave just yet. The rich cultural tapestry of Manipur had captivated her, and she longed to explore more of its lively festivals and diverse cuisines. With this newfound enthusiasm, she decided to extend her stay, eager to immerse herself further in the traditions that had already touched her heart. The journey wasn't over yet; there was still so much more to explore, taste, and experience in this magical land of Manipur.

****

VII

THE FEAST OF FLAVOURS

Another day began, accompanied by a feeling of excitement. Gatha had already seen glimpses of the land's culinary magic, but today, she was determined to indulge in an authentic Manipuri feast at Luxmi Kitchen, one of Imphal's most cherished eateries.

As she entered the restaurant with Thambal, the soothing aroma of slow-cooked vegetables, fermented delicacies, and scented steamed rice welcomed her. Tables were neatly arranged. The soft chatter of diners and the sound of cutlery clinking filled the air as she found a cosy corner to settle down.

"If you want to taste the authentic flavours of Manipur, Luxmi Kitchen is one of the best places," Thambal said with a smile.

"What would you recommend?" she asked eagerly.

"A Manipuri *thali* would be the best option," he suggested. "It has all the authentic dishes, such as *eromba, ooti, kangsoi, singju,* and of course, the famous black rice *kheer* for dessert. It is the perfect way to taste all the authentic dishes in one meal."

"That's exactly what I need," she agreed. "I will go for the thali."

Just then, a waiter approached them with a warm smile and handed her the menu.

"*Thagatchari* (a local Manipuri word for 'Thank you')! We

would love to taste Manipur's authentic flavours. So, we would like to order your special thali," she said.

The waiter's face lit up with a big smile. "Do you prefer a vegetarian thali or a non-vegetarian thali?" he asked, noting it down on a notepad.

"I want a non-vegetarian thali, please," she said with a smile.

"Excellent choice," the waiter said.

Soon, a beautifully presented plate of colourful dishes was placed before her.

"This is our traditional Manipuri thali," the waiter explained. "We begin with mild flavours and progress to the stronger ones."

Gatha gazed at the colourful platter of food in front of her, each dish meticulously arranged, promising a unique taste. There were nearly 11 mouth-watering varieties in the thali.

"Allow me to assist you," Thambal said. "Rice serves as the base of a Manipuri meal. So, start by taking a small portion of rice, and then mix it with your preferred side dishes, such as vegetables, fish, or pickles, savouring each flavour."

She first ate some rice with eromba, a simple yet flavourful dish made with mashed boiled vegetables, fermented fish (Ngari), and umorok chillies. A wave of intense flavours hit her—spicy, tangy, and umami—all at once. She coughed a little, feeling the heat of the king chilli spread through her senses.

An older lady at an adjacent table laughed. "That's the taste of Manipur!" she said. "If you can eat eromba, you are one of us now."

Gatha laughed, taking a sip of water to cool the burning sensation in her mouth.

Thambal also laughed. "Eromba was once a simple dish, made from available vegetables, but now, it is a dish that defines our cuisine," he said. "You should try ooti next to cut down the fiery sensation of eromba," he said, pointing to the dish.

She scooped a small portion of rice with ooti, a thick curry made with yellow peas, chives, and dill leaves. The subtle soothing, mild, creamy texture was comforting and earthy, balancing the fierceness of eromba.

"It is so different from eromba—mild, yet flavourful in its own way," Gatha said, enjoying another bite of it.

An elderly man at the next table nodded in agreement. "That's the beauty of a Manipuri thali. Every dish complements the other."

Thambal smiled. "And that's just the beginning. You still have kangsoi – a light curry that goes beautifully with rice."

She then tasted kangsoi, a traditional vegetable stew or curry including seasonal vegetables, onions, garlic, ginger, and *maroi* or leek, with rice. Its wholesome, earthy flavour, achieved through a simple cooking method, was so comforting that she lost herself in its warmth. The subtle aroma of maroi and the mild heat from the ginger made each spoonful feel like a soothing hug.

Gatha could feel the love and tradition blended in the meal. "I understand why it is not just food; it is comfort in a bowl," she said, taking another bite.

Thambal nodded and gestured towards the next item on her plate. "Now, you should taste *nga atoiba thongba,* Manipur's signature fish curry. It is a curry prepared with fish, simmered slowly with aromatic herbs, mustard leaves, and just a hint of spices."

The rich, slightly smoky taste of the fish melted in her mouth, perfectly complementing the subtle bitterness of the mustard leaves. The gentle warmth of the spices lingered, neither overpowering nor too mild—just the perfect balance.

"This is delicious," Gatha said. "The fish is so tender, and the flavours seem so fresh and natural."

Thambal smiled, "That's because it is cooked with minimal spices, allowing the natural taste of the ingredients to come through. I think you should also try the side dishes like *singju*. It is one of our most popular salads—crispy, spicy, and full of fresh flavours."

She looked down at the colourful mixture of finely chopped cabbage, lotus stem, and herbs, topped with roasted chickpea powder and a generous dash of chilli. She took a bite, the crunch of fresh vegetables instantly awakening her senses. The kick of the chilli and the tangy zest of lime unleashed a burst of flavours in her mouth.

"This is amazing!" she exclaimed, surprised. "I didn't expect a salad to have such a strong flavour. Even the salad is so delicious." She enjoyed the salad with some green chilli pickle.

"With the salad, you should taste champhut, which will balance the flavours," Thambal suggested.

Gatha tasted champhut, a simple vegetarian dish with a mild flavour and no spices. It is made with boiled vegetables like mustard leaves and shoots, carrots, cabbage, peas, bottle gourd, etc. Its natural flavours contrasted beautifully with the strong, tangy punch of singju and the spiciness of the green chilli pickle. This balance made champhut a soothing and essential part of a traditional Manipuri meal.

Gatha then tasted fried fish and shrimp pakoda, which were extremely crispy and flavourful. The marination was just perfect.

"This is so tasty!" she exclaimed, enjoying the contrast between the light champhut and the fried seafood.

Thambal looked at her and smiled. "And you can't settle for just one, can you?"

She laughed as she grabbed another shrimp pakoda, "You are absolutely right! The crispiness is irresistible!"

The waiter, who had been watching her reactions, smiled and said, "You are truly savouring Manipuri cuisine the way it is meant to be relished—flavours complementing one another, from the simplest boiled vegetables to the crispiest fried delicacies."

Gatha nodded, completely immersed in the culinary journey. "Each dish tells a unique story, but collectively, they create something even more special," she remarked.

Thambal pointed to the small bowl of *chak-hao kheer,* a sweet porridge made with black rice and milk. "And now, it's time for the most delightful and sweetest chapter of your meal."

Excited for the final taste, Gatha picked up her spoon, ready to savour the rich, creamy purple-coloured black rice kheer. She took a spoonful, allowing the flavours to melt on her tongue. It was nutty, aromatic, and deeply comforting.

"Chak-Hao Kheer is not just a dessert; it is a piece of our heritage. Black rice is special to us. It was once reserved only for the royalty," Thambal said.

"After tasting it, I understand why," Gatha replied, savouring another spoonful. "It is different from other desserts I have tasted before—rich yet light, simple yet bursting with flavours."

He nodded, "That's why it is the perfect way to end a Manipuri meal. After all the bold, spicy, and savoury dishes, this brings everything together in the sweetest way."

She leaned back, satiated, "This meal has been more than just food; it has been a journey through Manipur's culture, history, and traditions."

Just then, Thambal pointed towards the small bowl of salt on the table, "Use this to scrub your hands before washing," he said with a smile.

She was amazed to hear this, "Salt? I have never heard about it or done that before."

"It is an old practice," he explained. "After eating a meal with your hands, salt helps to remove oil and strong aromas from them. We still follow this tradition."

With curiosity, Gatha took a pinch of salt and rubbed it between her palms. "That's interesting! It feels different."

As she washed her hands, she was amazed by the little traditions that made the meal feel even more special. "I love learning these small but meaningful facts. Thank you so much for sharing this with me," she said gratefully.

Thambal nodded, "Food is never just about eating; it is about the experience, the traditions, and the stories we carry with us."

Gatha then finished her meal with a cup of *mangi mahi*, an acidic drink made with tamarind, usually consumed after a meal in Manipur. She felt a deep sense of connection. This was beyond just a culinary experience; it was a heartfelt embrace from the land itself.

Later in the evening, as they walked through the lively streets of Imphal, Thambal eagerly gestured towards a cart where an elderly man was roasting something over hot coals.

"Gatha, you need to taste this black corn," he said.

"Black corn?" Gatha asked with curiosity. She had heard about its availability in Peru, South America, but she was not aware of its availability in India, and that too in Manipur.

Thambal replied excitedly, "Yes! It is also known as *Chak Hao Makhai* in Manipur. It is not your ordinary corn; it has a distinct, slightly sweet and slightly nutty, earthy flavour and is rich in nutrients."

The vendor smiled warmly as he gave them each a roasted black corn.

Gatha took a bite, the smoky taste blending with the natural sweetness and nuttiness of the corn. "This is so delicious!" she exclaimed. "Manipur is full of hidden treasures. Everything here is unique and is narrating its own story."

As they kept exploring, enjoying their black corn, she understood that Manipur was revealing itself to her in the most beautiful way—through its people, its flavours, and its hospitality.

Later that night, as she sat beside her window, reflecting on the feast, she opened her journal and began to write:

The decision to extend this journey was absolutely the right one. Today, I didn't just taste Manipuri cuisine—I truly immersed myself in it. Every dish felt like a portal into the soul of this land, each flavour narrating its own story.

From the spicy Eromba that awakened my senses to the soothing warmth of Champhut, from the refreshing, crunchy Singju to the hearty, slow-cooked Nga Atoiba, the meal was a perfect balance of boldness and delicacy. The crispy shrimp pakoda added a delightful crunch, and just when I believed I had tasted it all, the rich, nutty sweetness of Chak-Hao Kheer completed the meal like a warm hug. Techniques new to me, like washing hands with salt—such a small and simple yet very important lesson—left me amazed.

Manipur's flavours are not just an experience on the palate; they are in the stories, in the hands that cook them, and in the hearts that share them. A meal here is not just food—it is a memory, a connection, and a legacy passed down through generations.

Sitting there in Luxmi Kitchen, sharing smiles and conversations with strangers who seemed like old friends, I realized something important—this journey was not just about places; it was also about the people, the stories, and the flavours that left a lasting imprint on my soul.

I will carry this taste of Manipur with me, always and forever.

With a smile, she closed her journal.

****

VIII

THE MANIPURI SPIRIT – DANCE, MUSIC, AND ART

As the rich taste of the Manipuri feast lingered in her mind, Gatha felt a deeper connection with the heart of Manipur—beyond its food, into the core of its artistic spirit. The land that spoke to her through its places and flavours now beckoned in the rhythm of its music, the grace of its dance, and the beauty of its art.

Dançe – The Rhythmic Expression of Devotion

The next morning, Thambal suggested they visit the iconic ISKCON Temple, also known as Sri Sri Radha Krishnachandra Temple, in Imphal, where a special *Ras Leela* performance was scheduled.

"Dance in Manipur is a spiritual and divine expression of faith," Thambal explained as they headed to the temple. "The most famous classical dance form of Manipur is Manipuri Raas Leela, a graceful performance depicting the love story of Radha and Krishna. This dance is known for its elegant hand gestures, delicate foot movements, and serene facial expressions, making it one of the most poetic dance forms in India. You cannot leave Manipur without experiencing this beautiful dance form."

"I am really excited to watch this spiritual dance form," Gatha said.

Upon arriving at the temple, she observed that, unlike other

ISKCON temples, the temple in Imphal showcased a distinctive, Tibetan-inspired architecture with a dome-like roof and was surrounded by sprawling gardens, exuding a sense of peace and divinity. This temple was a remarkable example of modern Hindu architecture.

"It feels like a fusion of different cultures," she said, capturing the temple's beauty and its surroundings on camera. "The Tibetan influence blends so beautifully with the traditional Hindu architecture."

Thambal smiled, happy at her obvious admiration, "Yes, that is what makes this temple special. Manipur has always been a crossroad of cultures. This temple reflects that beautifully."

As they walked through the temple, the rhythmic chanting of *"Hare Krishna"* echoed through the air, merging seamlessly with the sweet melody of traditional instruments. Devotees dressed in white and saffron wandered around, some immersed in prayers, while others prepared for the performance.

They took their seats, and shortly after, the sound of 'pung', a cylindrical, double-headed traditional Manipuri drum, resonated through the air, followed by the soft melody of flute and the rhythmic chime of anklets. The dancers appeared, lithe and graceful. Draped in their *potloi,* a cylindrical skirt of thick fabric adorned with sequins and mirrors, the women twirled elegantly, their hand movements precise yet fluid, their expressions reflecting deep devotion.

Gatha was mesmerized by the performance. "It feels as though I am watching a poem come alive," she said.

Thambal nodded in agreement. "Ras Leela is not just a simple dance form—it is an offering, a holy expression of love and devotion. This dance form captures the essence of Manipuri culture—elegant, spiritual, and deeply connected to tradition."

As the performance progressed, Gatha felt herself being carried away to a different world, where dance wasn't just for entertainment but a living force that linked the past with the present. She could sense something truly magical unfolding—a dance form intertwining devotion, narrative, and grace in a captivating display.

When the Ras Leela came to an end, there was pin-drop silence in the audience as a mark of respect for the art before applause broke out. Then another group of performers took the stage, dancing to a different rhythm.

"Is there another performance?" Gatha asked.

"This is *Nat Sankirtana*," Thambal replied. "It is another important dance form of Manipur. It is not just a dance but a ceremonial performance that combines singing, drumming, and dancing and is regarded as a cultural treasure and a form of worship."

The performers started singing and playing traditional instruments like the kartal and pung. They wore white dhotis and beautifully wrapped turbans. The rhythm was lively and soulful.

"Devotees express their love for Lord Krishna through music, dance, and storytelling during this ceremony, often portraying moments from the Radha-Krishna narrative, particularly focusing on Lord Krishna's early years and youth in Vrindavan," Thambal explained. "The interplay of singing, instruments, and movement creates a powerful emotional experience."

Gatha leaned forward, watching keenly, "This performance is quite different from Ras Leela, yet it is captivating. It feels more energetic and communal."

"True," he replied. "Nat Sankirtana is rhythmically powerful and engaging. In fact, UNESCO recognized it as an Intangible Cultural Heritage of Humanity in 2013. It symbolizes the spiritual heart of Vaishnavite practices in Manipur."

She felt goosebumps as the singers' voices rose together in a crescendo. The atmosphere was charged, yet profoundly sacred.

"This is extraordinary," she said with a surprised look on her face. "It resembles the heartbeat of Manipur."

He looked at her warmly. "You are absolutely correct. In Manipur, music and dance embody poetry in motion."

As the last echoes of the pung faded into the air, the performers moved with grace, akin to the flowing rivers of Loktak, their expressions reflecting ancient stories handed down through generations. Fascinated, Gatha watched them dance as though transformed into celestial beings. The performance was more than just a visual feast; it was an awakening. At that moment, she realized that it was not merely a retelling of myths but a sacred tribute, a vibrant memory interwoven with rhythm and movement. The enchantment had revealed itself, leaving a mark on her spirit.

Music – The Soul of Manipuri Culture

After the mesmerizing Ras Leela performance, she felt a strong desire to explore more of Manipur's artistic legacy. Thambal suggested visiting a small music workshop tucked away in one of Imphal's quiet lanes. As they made their way through the lanes, the faint sound of a stringed instrument guided them toward the workshop's wooden entrance.

Inside, the air was filled with the warm, earthy scent of aged wood, accompanied by the soft buzz of instruments being tuned. Musicians sat cross-legged on the floor, deeply focused on their practice, while an elderly guru supervised closely.

"Music in Manipur is a powerful medium for storytelling and devotion," Thambal said, pride evident in his voice. "It is deeply rooted in the Vaishnavite traditions that shape the area, along with indigenous tribal practices. The classical music of Manipur, inspired by the Ras Leela, is rich in devotion and often dedicated to Lord Krishna."

Gatha listened intently, absorbing every word. "What are Manipur's traditional instruments?" she asked, curiosity shining in her eyes.

He pointed to the musicians. "Instruments such as the 'pena', a one-stringed bowed lute, are symbolic of Manipuri folk music and play a crucial role in rituals and storytelling. Other traditional instruments include the 'pung', the 'shankha' (conch), the 'kartal' and 'manjira' (small cymbals), and the bamboo flute."

Just then, the eerily beautiful melodies of the pena resonated through the workshop. A young girl, seated on the floor, played with intense focus, her fingers skillfully moving, while an elderly guru guided her.

Gatha, captivated by the sound, asked the guru, "The pena has such a soulful, ancient essence. What makes it sound so special?"

With a warm smile and eyes reflecting years of wisdom, the guru replied, "The pena is the heartbeat of our music. Our ancestors played it to narrate tales of bravery and wisdom. Today, we use it to preserve our culture. Each note carries the legacy of our land."

As she explored the workshop further, her gaze landed on an instrument displayed on the wall—a pung, its shiny wooden exterior glistening under the soft light. She remembered seeing it used in the Ras Leela performance. A musician picked it up and began to play, his fingers sliding smoothly across the drum, creating an intricate rhythm that filled the room with energy.

"The pung is one of our oldest instruments," he explained, striking it gently. "It is not simply played; it is performed. It accompanies our traditional dances."

Gatha closed her eyes briefly, allowing the rhythms of the pung and the melancholic melody of the pena to wash over her. "These instruments are so soothing to the ears," she said, gently swaying to the rhythm.

The musician nodded in agreement, "This is one of our well-known folk songs. Folk music in Manipur is deeply connected to our way of life. We have *Khullang Eshei* (village songs), *Lai Haraoba* songs, which are associated with our customary festival that pays tribute to our deities, and *Thabal Chongba* songs that accompany our famous moonlight dance performed during the Yaoshang (Holi) Festival."

Gatha opened her eyes, gratitude reflecting in them, "What I feel is that music in Manipur is not just sound; it is an emotion, a history, and an identity," she said.

"Yes, and this evening, you have experienced the essence of our land," Thambal replied with a proud smile, seeing how deeply she had connected with Manipur's musical tradition.

As they stepped out of the workshop, the echoes of the instruments remained in her heart, a tune that would linger long after departing from Manipur.

Art – The Visual Representation of Tradition

As they left the music workshop, the rhythmic sounds of the pena and pung continued to resonate in her thoughts. However, Thambal still had more to reveal about the richness of Manipur's legacy.

"Music is just one part of our heritage," he said as they walked through the quiet lanes of Imphal. "Our arts—handwoven fabrics, intricate handicrafts, and paintings—are equally important. Art in Manipur is a reflection of its vibrant cultural history."

Curious and excited, Gatha trailed behind him to an artisan's workshop, small and cosy, where the scent of fresh bamboo and cotton filled the air. Inside, three elderly women perched on wooden stools, their hands expertly weaving delicate designs on a classic loin loom.

One of the artisans, a woman with deep, wise eyes, looked up and smiled. "Welcome," she said. "You have arrived at the right time. We are weaving a unique phanek today."

Gatha observed with intrigue as vivid strands of red, green, and gold were woven together into a captivating design. "This is lovely," she murmured, gliding her fingers across the textile.

"The phanek is more than just clothing," Thambal explained. "For Manipuri women, it symbolizes strength, identity, pride, and tradition. Each design narrates a story—some are drawn from nature, while others are inspired by mythology or history."

Unlike the others, the phanek held up by the elderly woman had a particularly lustrous and delicate sheen. "This one is made from pure lotus silk. It is among the rarest fabrics in the world," she said.

Gatha's eyes widened in surprise. "Lotus silk? I didn't know there was a fabric made from a flower."

"Yes, and Manipur is one of the few places in the world where you will find it," Thambal replied with a smile. "The threads are manually pulled from the stems of lotus flowers cultivated in Loktak Lake and other wetlands. Producing even a small piece of fabric requires thousands of stems."

The woman stroked the silk softly with her fingers. "It is a delicate and time-consuming task. The material is lightweight, breathable, and has a natural shine. It is believed to have spiritual purity and is often used for special ceremonies."

Gatha extended her hand, tracing the fabric with respect. "It feels vibrant, as if it carries the essence of the water and the hands that crafted it."

"Exactly," Thambal replied gently. "That is what makes it sacred."

The soft humming of the loom resonated throughout the workshop, yet Gatha's focus remained on the shining phanek crafted from lotus silk. Curiously, she turned to the elderly woman and asked, "Could you demonstrate how this silk is created? It is unlike anything I have seen to date."

The woman smiled warmly. "Yes, certainly. It begins not in the workshop, but in the water."

A middle-aged woman, draped in a plain cotton wrap, called them over. "Are you here to learn about lotus silk?" she asked with a smile.

"Yes," Gatha replied. "Turning a flower into fabric seems like magic."

The woman said, "My dear, it is more work than magic, but it certainly feels special."

She grabbed a green lotus stem that was still wet with lake water. "First, we gather thousands of freshly cut stems. We work quickly to prevent the fibres from drying out."

She effortlessly made a small cut near the base of the stem and tugged gently. From the cut came thin, nearly undetectable, silvery white sticky threads.

"This is the heart of the silk," she said, gently placing the strands on a plain surface. "We extract threads from each stem like this. This is delicate work that requires patience."

Gatha watched in amazement as another woman gradually shaped the sticky fibres into a continuous thread on a smooth wooden board.

"We never roll them by machine; we roll them together by

hand," said the second woman. "If we pull too quickly, the thread breaks easily. This part requires years of practice."

Gatha asked, "How many stems are needed to produce enough thread for one phanek?"

"Approximately 120,000 to 160,000 lotus stems," Thambal replied. "That is why it is so rare and valuable."

The first woman nodded. "Even after extraction, the fibres must be dried, spun, and sometimes mixed gently with cotton to add strength. However, pure lotus silk retains its lightness and airiness while displaying a soft, natural lustre."

The second woman added, "Lotus silk is more than just fabric; it is a gift that carries the spirit of Loktak."

"Do many people know about this special fabric?" Gatha asked.

Thambal shook his head. "Not yet. Manipur's lotus silk is still a hidden gem, but it is starting to gain recognition in recent years."

Gatha nodded. "This will surely gain recognition in no time. This is not just weaving but devotion."

The woman smiled. "Each thread narrates a story – from the lotus flourishing in muddy water to the hands that carefully unveil its beauty. That is what transforms it into art."

As the women continued their work, Gatha's gaze fell upon a completed phanek showcased on a nearby bamboo rack. It shone delicately, golden threads intricately woven into a light ivory foundation, the fabric seemingly radiating an internal glow.

She stepped closer, mesmerized. "Is this phanek made of lotus silk too?"

"Yes," the elderly woman replied. "This one took more than two months to complete. It contains no cotton blends and is composed solely of pure lotus fibres."

"This is beautiful," Gatha said admiringly, running her fingers over the pattern, the fabric feeling exceptionally soft beneath her touch. "I have never seen anything like this."

The woman looked at her thoughtfully. "This would look good on you."

Gatha blushed, moved by the warmth of the compliment. She said, "I want to buy it. Not just as a souvenir, but as something sacred."

Thambal smiled. "Then you should definitely buy it."

With skilful elegance, the woman lifted the phanek, folded it, and wrapped it in a handloom cotton cloth pouch. "Take it with blessings," she said. "May it remind you of the quiet strength of the lotus."

As Gatha accepted the package, she bowed gently with her palms together. "Thank you for this and for allowing me to witness something so precious."

The woman smiled and replied, "Carry our stories with you."

Gatha held the phanek close to her chest, already imagining the day she would wear it. Suddenly, her gaze shifted to the walls of the workshop, where detailed Thang-Ta paintings and scroll paintings adorned the space. These artworks, she understood, were not merely artistic expressions but carried deep spiritual and historical significance.

Moving forward into the next room, they saw a young artisan carefully carving elaborate designs onto a piece of black stone pottery, a rare craft specific to Manipur. He

raised his head and gestured towards his work. "This technique has been passed down for generations," he said. "This pottery is primarily black in colour, reflecting indigenous traditions. Unlike regular pottery in other parts of India, we don't use a potter's wheel. Everything is moulded by hand, polished with bamboo, and then baked in an open fire."

The precision and patience each artist displayed were astounding. Gatha marvelled at it. "This pottery is truly made with a unique technique, and each piece has a soul," she said, picking up a beautifully completed pot.

Thambal smiled. "Yes, because everything—our music, our dance, our art—comes from our history, our beliefs, and our love for this land."

As they moved ahead, Gatha noticed an elderly man sitting on a wooden stool, skilfully crafting an exquisite cane basket with practised ease. His wrinkled hands moved expertly, intertwining bamboo strands with accuracy to form a detailed design. The half-complete basket lay in his lap, its curved shape already taking form.

She paused to watch him work, fascinated by the rhythmic movement of his hands. "Your skills are amazing," she said.

The elderly man glanced up with a warm smile. "Thank you, child," he replied. "Weaving baskets is an age-old tradition in Manipur. The art of weaving baskets is an age-old tradition in Manipur. Our ancestors crafted these not only for transporting goods but also as symbols of prosperity."

Thambal picked up a basket—a sturdy, intricately woven piece featuring elegant floral designs carved into the surface. "It is commonly used in ceremonies and celebrations," he explained. "Every pattern has its own meaning—some symbolize nature, while others signify prosperity."

Gatha traced her fingers over the surface of the basket, appreciating the artistry. "This is incredible; so much talent goes into something so basic yet so significant," she said.

The artisan laughed. "This might look simple, but weaving

requires patience and precision. Every strand has to be positioned just right, or the whole structure loses strength."

She smiled as she observed him continue weaving, every movement intentional and consistent, a quiet tribute to the traditions inherited through generations.

As they moved forward, she said to Thambal, "I never understood how intricately woven art is with daily life here. It is not solely about aesthetics or beauty; it is about culture, history, and identity."

He agreed, "Exactly. That's what makes it unique. Whether it is music, textiles, pottery, or basket weaving, every craft carries the spirit of Manipur."

With every step, she felt a deeper bond with the people and their art—an unspoken language of legacy that echoed throughout Manipur.

As they stepped outside into the refreshing night breeze, she took a final look at the beautiful artworks around her. She realized that in Manipur, art represented a form of language, a heritage, and a lifestyle.

A Reflection of the Manipuri Soul

With each step further into Manipur's artistic world, she felt herself becoming a part of its eternal narratives, where tradition and creativity flowed together in flawless unity.

That night, while sitting by her window, she took out her journal and wrote:

And so, the choice to prolong this adventure was absolutely correct. After the feast of flavours, today I have indulged in the soul of Manipur – its music, dance, and art. From the celestial movements of Ras Leela and Nat Sankirtan to the resonating rhythms of the pung, from the mesmerizing tunes of the pena to the intricate patterns of potteries, handlooms, and crafts, each component holds a narrative, a legacy.

I also learned about lotus silk, which is handcrafted by extracting the fibres from the stems of lotus flowers that bloom in Loktak Lake and other wetlands. I witnessed the journey of a flower transformed into fabric. Moreover, when I held that phanek, made from thousands of lotus stems, I wasn't simply holding fabric; I was holding the soul of this place, crafted with love, tradition, and power.

Manipur doesn't just preserve its traditions – it lives them every single day. Here, art binds individuals together through a shared history and culture in a rhythm that is indistinguishable from life.

I came here as a stranger, but now I feel like I am a part of it—the sounds, colours, and textures of this place embrace my spirit. And I know that when I leave, I will always carry a part of Manipur's soul with me – forever.

She leaned back, closed her journal, and looked out at the quiet night. As sleep slowly took over, she realized that when the time came to depart, Manipur would not be just another place she had visited. It would become a story she would share for years, a tune that would play in the background of her heart, and a memory etched in her mind.

With that thought, she surrendered to dreams filled with twirling dancers, rhythmic beats, and the heartfelt spirit of a place that had changed her forever.

****

IX

THE FESTIVAL OF LIFE

Although Gatha's visit to Manipur was nothing short of incredible, her last day arrived amid the lavish festivities of the Sangai Festival, as her trip coincided with it.

"The Sangai Festival is an annual cultural event in Manipur," Thambal explained. "It honours the state›s rich heritage and its state animal, the Sangai deer. It is usually celebrated from November 21st to 30th. The festival derives its name from the Sangai, or brow-antlered deer, which is a rare species native only to Manipur and is designated as the state animal."

"That sounds interesting," Gatha said. "What is the significance of this festival?"

"The festival aims to promote Manipur as a tourism destination to the world and showcase unity among the different communities of Manipur," he explained. "The Sangai Festival has developed into a major platform for Manipur to exhibit its diverse heritage and has gained recognition as the most spectacular celebration in the state."

Eager to make the most of her last few hours in Manipur, she ventured into the heart of the celebrations. The streets buzzed with excitement, the aroma of traditional foods filled the air, and the rhythmic beats of folk music echoed all around. The streets were lined with stalls selling beautiful bamboo crafts, handmade jewellery, and intricately woven textiles.

As they strolled along, Gatha noticed a booth selling beautifully carved wooden souvenirs. A wooden sculpture of the Sangai deer stood out among them."How much does this Sangai cost?" she asked, pointing to it.

"Fifteen hundred rupees," the vendor replied.

Without hesitation, she purchased it. With its elegant and intricate carvings, the wooden Sangai would serve as an excellent memento of her stay in Manipur.

The sound of pungcholom drumming drew them to an outdoor stage as they explored deeper. The dancers, dressed in colourful traditional clothing, moved gracefully, their gestures narrating stories of love and bravery. A young boy stood beside her, gazing in amazement.

"Do you like this dance form?" she asked him.

He nodded. "Yes! I want to dance like them one day."

She laughed. "I am sure you will! You simply need to keep practising."

Thambal and Gatha headed to the food stalls, driven by a desire to taste local dishes. She was lured by the aroma of freshly made eromba and relished every bite. She then tried chak-hao kheer and enjoyed its unique flavour.

"Do you like it?" Thambal asked, seeing her happy expression.

"It's delicious!" she exclaimed.

The seller smiled and said, "You should take some black rice home with you."

She agreed and bought some black rice to take with her.

Thambal asked her, "Are you enjoying this festival?"

"Yes. It is amazing," she replied. "I wish I could stay longer in Manipur to celebrate it."

He smiled. "Manipur celebrates many beautiful festivals."

"Like what?" she asked with curiosity.

"Have you heard about 'Kang'?" he asked as they walked by a booth selling miniature chariots, Jagannath paintings, and idols.

She shook her head and said, "No, can you tell me about it?"

"Kang is the Manipuri name for *Rath Yatra,* which is celebrated all over the world. It is dedicated to Lord Jagannath. We pull a huge chariot through the streets while chanting devotional songs," he explained.

"That sounds incredible," she said. "What other festivals are celebrated in Manipur?"

"There is one festival called 'Cheiroba', which is the Manipuri New Year," he continued. "Families clean their houses, prepare special meals, and ascend a hill or a small mound to symbolize striving for greater heights in life."

She listened intently. "That seems like a fantastic way to kick off the year."

"Then there's 'Yaoshang', which is Manipur's version of the Holi festival," he added. "It is a spring festival celebrated for five days straight. The grand festival includes 'Thabal Chongba', a traditional dance where boys and girls hold hands and dance in a circle under the moonlight. Different events take place in different parts of Manipur, like traditional sports such as marathons, cultural performances, and vibrant celebrations with colours—similar to Holi—where people spray colours on each other, along with grand feasts organized in local communities."

"That sounds lovely. I wish I could witness the beauty of Yaoshang," she said, imagining the vibrant celebration.

Thambal nodded. "And finally, there's also 'Emoinu', a festival honouring the goddess of prosperity. We light lamps and offer her food to seek her blessings."

"That sounds so peaceful," she said with a warm smile.

They stopped for a moment at a stall offering treats. She

tasted some leaf-wrapped sticky rice. As they moved along, they encountered a group of individuals elegantly dressed in traditional clothing – vibrant phaneks, intricate headpieces, and luxurious shawls woven with tribal patterns. Gatha couldn't resist asking for a photograph. The group greeted her warmly, laughing and striking confident poses. Thambal took a picture after one of the women wrapped a scarf around Gatha's shoulders and exclaimed, "Now you look like one of us!" The moment was more than just a snapshot; it was a memory she would treasure for a lifetime.

As they continued, her eyes sparkled with revived curiosity. "Are there even more festivals celebrated in Manipur?" she asked, eager to learn more about the state's rich culture.

"Oh, yes! Another important celebration is 'Lai Haraoba'. It is a festival during which we pay tribute to our gods and ancestors with traditional music, dancing, and ceremonies. It is a wonderful display of our vibrant cultural heritage," he explained.

"That sounds spiritual," she replied.

"The Naga tribes' seed-sowing festival, 'Lui Ngai Ni', is also significant. This is a time for communities to unite, rejoice with folk dances, songs, and rituals, and pray for a prosperous harvest," he added.

"That is such a lovely way to celebrate nature," she said.

He continued, "'Heikru Hitongba' is another festival celebrated in Manipur. It is a unique boat race that takes place in a narrow canal. It's thrilling to see the long boats zip across the water while spectators cheer from the sidelines."

"That must be exciting to watch!" she exclaimed.

"Additionally, we also celebrate Ramzan Eid and Christmas with the same level of joy. During Eid, people share sweets like *sewai*, break their fast with feasts, and pray in mosques. On

Christmas, people gather for midnight mass, and churches are beautifully adorned."

"That's fantastic! It is incredible how Manipur celebrates such a wide range of festivals," she said, smiling.

"There's also 'Ningol Chakouba'," he continued. "It is a special festival where married women return to their parents' house for a lavish meal. It's a lovely way to strengthen familial ties."

Her eyes lit up. "That sounds so heartwarming—a festival dedicated to celebrating family love."

He agreed. "Then there's 'Kut', the Kuki-Chin-Mizo tribes' festival that takes place after the harvest. It is a Thanksgiving celebration featuring a community feast, folk music, and colourful dance performances."

"That must be an incredibly joyful celebration!" she said.

"Additionally, we also host the 'Shirui Lily Festival'," Thambal continued. "It honours the rare Shirui Lily, which only blooms in the hills of Ukhrul. The festival includes nature walks to admire the beautiful flowers, cultural performances, and music concerts."

"A celebration for a flower? That's truly one of a kind!" she exclaimed in awe.

"Yes, the beauty of Manipur is deeply linked to nature, traditions, and festivities. We celebrate with welcoming hearts and a strong sense of tradition," he said proudly.

Gatha smiled. "I wish I could stay longer to fully immerse myself in all of this."

A sudden explosion of applause drew their attention as they strolled deeper into the lively surroundings of the Sangai Festival. Thambal gestured to a vast, open ground where a traditional polo game was in progress. With their bamboo mallets skilfully swinging to hit the ball, the riders galloped across the field on strong Manipuri ponies, while the audience buzzed with excitement. The energy was contagious.

Amazed by the players' speed and coordination, Gatha asked, "Is this...polo?"

"Yes," he replied, smiling proudly. "This isn't just any polo, though; it's 'Sagol Kangjei', the original form of polo that originated right here in Manipur. It's more than a sport to us – it's a legacy."

He described how the Manipuri pony, renowned for its strength, agility, and endurance, has been crucial to this traditional sport for centuries. The game was first played by nobles and soldiers, and it was closely linked to the region's martial and religious customs. She observed the impressive bond between the riders and their ponies as they rode bareback or with minimal equipment. Simple, traditional clothing and raw, passionate talent replaced glamorous uniforms. The rhythmic gallop of the ponies, the clack of the mallet hitting the ball, and the audience's excited cheers created an atmosphere that was both exhilarating and profoundly cultural.

"I had no idea polo came from here," Gatha said, her gaze fixed on the field. "This is intense yet graceful."

Thambal sighed. "The majority of people don't know about this. However, it is one of Manipur's oldest and most cherished sports. For this reason, it is always a memorable part of the Sangai Festival; it serves as a reminder of our origins. Papal Kangjeibung is the oldest polo ground in the world, located in the heart of Imphal."

As the game continued, her admiration grew, not only for the sport itself but also for the proud spirit of the land that had supported it for so many years. Leaning against the bamboo railing, she was engrossed in the view. "It is incredible how each aspect of this festival—cuisine, artwork, music, sports—weaves together the soul of Manipur."

He smiled. "Exactly. The Sangai Festival is like a living museum of who we are."

As night fell, the festival site transformed into a dazzling display of light and sound. The grand celebration included a stunning fireworks display that lit up the night sky with a rainbow of colours. Gatha felt a surge of gratitude as she stood among the happy throngs.

Thambal let out a joyful sigh. "It is always this lovely."

She smiled. "It certainly is. I feel fortunate to have had this experience on my last day here."

"So, you will return tomorrow, right?" he asked.

With a big smile, she responded, "I believe a part of me will forever remain here."

She took one last glance around, imprinting every detail in her memory as the final burst of fireworks faded into the darkness. She would always treasure her farewell to Manipur, knowing the spirit of the Sangai Festival had made a lasting impression on her heart.

That evening, in her room, she opened her journal and began writing:

"What a day it has been on my last day in Manipur! The Sangai Festival was a mesmerizing event, full of life, tradition, colour, and vibrancy. Everything was flawless, from the lively dances and heartfelt music to the friendly locals and delicious cuisine. I will always remember this magical place thanks to the wooden Sangai I purchased as a souvenir. Today, I gained valuable insight into Manipuri

culture, and even though I am leaving tomorrow, I am certain that I will always carry a part of Manipur within me – always and forever."

She placed her journal next to her bed with a satisfied sigh and fell asleep peacefully.

****

X
THE FAREWELL – A CHANGED PERSPECTIVE

The last morning in Imphal started gently, with golden sunlight caressing the hilltops and filtering through the mist like a farewell blessing. Gatha stood on the balcony of Hotel Imphal. She had come to Manipur seeking a story but found a revelation instead. Ready to depart, she gathered her belongings and came downstairs for breakfast.

Transformation Through Connection

Gatha kept on thinking about the previous night—about the Sangai Festival with fireworks lighting up the sky and dancers twirling like spirits of the land. The colours, rhythms, and whispers of tradition had awakened something in her. What had started as a simple assignment—an article for a travel magazine—had evolved into something deeper, something sacred.

Thambal approached her with a warm cup of laal cha. His steps were slow and deliberate, as if he, too, felt the weight of farewell in the air.

When Gatha first arrived in Manipur, she had felt out of place—a traveller in an alien land. The landscapes were vastly different from the bustling streets of her city life, and the people, though warm, friendly, and inviting, seemed to live by different rhythms and rules. She had arrived as a tourist, excited to explore, but she was departing as someone transformed—someone who had experienced the resilience, beauty, and intricacy of both the land and its people.

They drove towards the airport. As she gazed out one final time at the scenery she had grown to cherish—the rolling hills, waving grasses, and distant bird calls—memories came rushing back like a tide that couldn't be held back. She thought of Kangla Fort and its silent strength, the echo of footsteps in the alleys of Ima Keithel, and the flickering bonfire during cultural evenings. From the phumdis of Loktak Lake to the Sangai deer of Keibul Lamjao National Park, from the INA Memorial in Moirang to the Khongjam War Memorial in Thoubal, she had immersed herself in the rich history of Manipur. She recalled the monoliths, cherry blossoms, and lotus silk, along with the earthen warmth of Andro's traditional pottery, where ancient hands shaped stories into clay, and the bustling streets of Imphal. From the remote hills of Ukhrul to the spiritual heart of Tamenglong, she had engaged deeply with the culture, history, and landscapes of the region. She remembered the smiles of strangers who had become friends. She also thought of Thambal and his quiet companionship, and of the numerous cups of *laal cha* that had warmed both her hands and her soul. Yet, more than the places, it was the perspective that had transformed her.

"You have changed a lot," Thambal said.

"Really?" she asked with a smile, though her gaze was far away.

"You once observed everything as an outsider—intrigued yet reserved. Now you see it the way we cherish this land. You see us," he replied.

She agreed. "For me, it is not just a place anymore; it is a heartbeat."

Throughout the expedition, Thambal, her ever-patient guide,

provided insight into the area›s history, culture, and the strong bond between its people and the land. Over the course of their travels, she had come to realize that Manipur was more than just a place; it was a living story that had unfolded over centuries. Something had changed within her as a result of their connection, which had developed through the gradual intertwining of tales and silences. Through Thambal, she had discovered that Manipur was not merely a place to be described in words, but rather a spirit to be felt.

A Journey of Self-Discovery

Gatha had worn her city like armour—quick, doubtful, and resolute—when she first arrived in Manipur. However, as the days went by, she found herself softened by the sounds of the pena, the flavour of fermented bamboo shoots, and the laughter of villagers celebrating around bonfires.

Gatha stood at the edge of Imphal Airport, her suitcase beside her and her heart full of emotions, as the morning fog softly enveloped the hills. The soft hum of a distant flight broke the silence, yet inside her, there was a stillness she had never experienced before. She had arrived in Manipur as a visitor, unsure, but she was departing as an evolved person—her heart open, her spirit awakened, and her soul forever influenced by the land she was now preparing to leave.

"I came here to write a story," she murmured to herself, "but it seems like the story found me instead."

Thambal laughed. "That is how Manipur, is. You don't just write about it; you become part of it."

She had come searching for stories but discovered significance. She had planned to observe a culture but instead became a part of it. What started out as a study of geography had turned into an introspective quest. She had discarded preconceptions like an old shedding skin and embraced the unexpected—language barriers that dissolved into laughter, unfamiliar dishes that became favourites, and traditions that awakened a newfound reverence in her.

Standing there, ready to leave, she realized she was no longer looking at Manipur from the outside. She carried it within her now, etched into her memories and woven into her consciousness. The tales, melodies, and smiles had fused into the fabric of her existence.

Saying Goodbye

The announcement for boarding echoed softly through the airport speakers, jolting Gatha out of her thoughts. She faced Thambal, her throat tightening with the ache of departure. They didn't say anything for a while. The silence between them felt full, like the stillness before the final note of a beautiful song.

"I don't know how to say goodbye," she said in a tremulous voice.

"There is no need to say goodbye," he replied, looking at her with a smile. "Some people… and some places… they don't leave you."

She nodded, the tears in her eyes surprising her. "Will you keep walking those paths? Sharing those stories?"

"Yes, I will," he replied. "And you? Are you going to write about us?"

She smiled through the lump in her throat. "I will try my best. But it won't be just an article. It will be something different. Something real."

He reached into his bag and took out a small fabric pouch, gently placing it on her palm. Inside was a dried flower from the

Sangai Festival grounds, delicate yet preserved.

"This is a small token from Manipur," he said. "To remind you of your time here."

She tightened her grip on the pouch, holding it like a talisman. "I appreciate it, Thambal. For all that you've done, thank you."

He gave her a small bow, a gesture of respect. "Travel safely, Gatha. May the story guide you, just as this land has guided us."

As she walked towards the gate, she did not look back—not because she was not leaving anything behind, but because she was carrying so much with her. And as she proceeded towards the plane, she realized she wasn't saying goodbye to Manipur; she was saying thank you.

The Departure

From her window seat, she watched as the landscape of Manipur slowly receded beneath the clouds. The hills that had once seemed unfamiliar now looked like old friends bidding farewell. She gently pressed her forehead against the glass, the pouch with the dried flower cradled in her palm. It felt like she was saying goodbye to a version of herself rather than just a place. The woman who had arrived was no longer the one departing.

As the plane ascended, memories flashed through her mind like lanterns in the dusk. Each moment had engraved itself upon her, like poetry she hadn't known how to read until now.

On the flight back to Pune, she opened her notebook and placed it on her lap. Its pages were no longer filled with notes but with reflections. The margins brimmed with emotions, fragments of local proverbs shared by Thambal, and sketches of the land and its people. It was not just a journalist's diary; it was a guide to her personal evolution. The last line she wrote in the journal was:

"In Manipur, I didn't just find stories—I found myself."

And as the clouds cleared below her, she finally understood that some departures are not endings but beginnings whispered softly by the land you leave behind.

"Goodbye, Manipur," she whispered. "Or maybe...see you again."

Closing her journal, with her heart full and her eyes shining, she leaned back—not away from Manipur, but into the world, carrying a piece of its spirit forever hers.

Epilogue

Manipur Diaries is not just a travelogue; it is a heartfelt tribute to the beauty, resilience, and culture of Manipur. The novel inspires a deeper appreciation for cultural preservation and the transformative power of travel. Through vivid landscapes, genuine voices, and deep personal insights, it captures the essence of a land often overlooked yet immensely rich in heritage and spirit.

Memories tend to soften over time, leaving only their core as the vivid details of an experience blur. However, some places and people remain etched in our hearts forever. For Gatha, Manipur was one such place. It did not quietly fade into the shadows of her life. Through her journey to Manipur, she realized that travel is not simply a tour; it is about exploring hidden treasures and stories with a transformed perspective.

Even back in her bustling city with glass towers and bright lights, work deadlines, and brief conversations, Gatha carried Manipur within her. It was not expressed in bold statements or travel stories shared online, but it existed in her memories. In quiet moments, Manipur returned to her—not as a destination, but as a feeling.

Manipur taught her to observe, not just look. She learned to appreciate the care with which an artisan hand-wove a basket, the skill of a married woman creating beautiful pottery, the patience involved in preparing smoked bamboo fish curry over an open flame, and the stories passed down through generations, embodied in each step of the traditional dance forms, their rhythms echoing ancient history.

There were days when Gatha woke up early, even before sunrise, an instinct she had unknowingly adopted. In those peaceful hours, she recalled the mists over valley, the clouds caressing the mountain peaks like lovers sharing secrets. She would prepare a cup of laal cha, not exactly like the one she had enjoyed in Manipur, but enough to transport her back there, lost in her thoughts.

On her desk, she kept the hand-carved wooden Sangai souvenir from the Sangai Festival. It was not just a keepsake; it was a guardian, a silent sentinel of her memories. Its curved antlers reminded her of nature's grace and the delicate balance between progress and conservation. Nearby, her journal rested, its pages worn and delicate. Inside were scribbled thoughts, reflections, recipes, and names she refused to forget. There were sketches, too—a fisherman casting his net into Loktak Lake at sunrise, a performer dancing in the Sangai Festival, a woman selling cane baskets at Ima Keithel, and Thambal gesturing to Sangai deer at Keibul Lamjao National Park. The diary also held pressed cherry blossoms, faded but eternal, like the lessons she carried home—resilience in stillness, strength in softness, and beauty in simplicity.

These were not just memories; they were talismans. Manipur taught her that the most profound journeys are measured not in miles but in moments of connection—with the land, with people, and most importantly, with oneself.

She didn't share her experiences of Manipur with everyone;

some things are too sacred to be reduced to mere stories. But when she spoke of it, her voice changed and softened—like a song remembered or a prayer whispered.

Most of the time, she would share stories of Manipur with her family, close friends, and colleagues, inspiring them to explore and appreciate the diversity of India. Her friends observed the change in her tone and perspective, and they listened more intently. She told them about the floating phumdis of Loktak, the Sangai of Keibul Lamjao, Asia's largest market run entirely by women, the hoisting of the first Indian flag in Moirang, mysteries in the hills of Ukhrul and Tamenglong, the sacred caves of Tamenglong and Churachandpur, the hidden gems of Manipur, its beautiful dance forms, musical instruments, handicrafts, cuisines, and festivals. She recounted the laughter shared with strangers and the silences that spoke just as loudly—silences conveying history, sacrifices, and peace. This was a story she would carry with her forever.

The travel journal was not what Gatha brought back from Manipur; it was a new way of living. She began volunteering with local environmental projects, utilizing insights gained from her experiences in Manipur. She also cooked differently, infusing Northeastern flavours and principles into her everyday cuisine, such as minimizing waste. Additionally, she initiated a storytelling group, allowing voices from different corners of India to be heard, honoured, and shared. When questioned about her motivation, she consistently replied, "Because every culture holds wisdom. You simply need to listen with your heart."

In her published article, she wrote:

"Manipur was not just a journey I completed; it was a journey that completed me."

And this was absolutely true. Manipur had changed her

perspective forever. Her soul had been reshaped by Manipur's hills, caves, and waters, its cuisines and festivals, its people and stories. She was not merely a person who had undertaken a journey to Manipur; she was a person moulded by it. As a result, she continued to live a life that was more thoughtful and grounded. She no longer found joy in the endless pursuits of her bustling city. Sharing meals, recalling stories, and exchanging smiles—these were the things that truly mattered.

Some places don't just change your view of the world; they change you. And for Gatha, Manipur was not just a chapter in her story; it was the turning point.

Manipur Diaries leaves behind not only memories but the heartbeat of a soul forever touched.

Acknowledgements

Despite being written from Gatha's point of view, this journey across Manipur is a heartfelt tribute to the land, its people, and the spirit that embodies every tradition, hill, and lake.

To the people of Manipur—thank you for your warmth, stories, and unwavering hospitality. The real heartbeat of this narrative has been your resilience, grace, and cultural diversity. You welcomed a stranger and turned her into a part of your tapestry. For that, I am deeply grateful.

To the storytellers, Reena Didi, artists, dancers, chefs, and guides—thank you for sharing a part of yourselves. Your presence made this journey more than mere travel; it became a transformation. These pages came to life with every shared recipe, folk song, dance step, and whispered legend.

A special thank you to the guardians of history—the curators, historians, and keepers of sacred spaces who continue to preserve and share the legacy of Manipur for future generations. Your dedication made it possible for me to follow Gatha's journey through stories once etched in stone or only spoken in hushed tones.

To the land itself—Loktak Lake, with its floating phumdis and misty mornings; the hills of Koubru and Shirui, standing tall like ancient sentinels; the sacred caves echoing forgotten chants; the unexplored gems of Manipur; and the lively streets of Imphal that pulsate with rhythm and resilience—thank you for your silent lessons, patience, and poetry. You were a guide, a soul, a character, and not just a backdrop.

To my beloved husband—thank you for being my unwavering pillar. Your encouragement through every late night, your faith when I doubted myself, and your quiet strength formed the foundation on which this book was built. You reminded me, time and again, that stories like these matter.

To our precious daughter—even in your infancy, you gave me purpose and perspective. Although I carried this story through my pregnancy and into the whirlwind of new motherhood, your presence never held me back. Instead, you motivated me to keep going and complete this book with more enthusiasm than I could have imagined. You reminded me that creation, in any form, is an act of love and courage.

To my mother—thank you for sitting with me, reading through drafts, and helping me shape this story with your suggestions and honest feedback. You helped refine each chapter with your constant encouragement. This book carries a touch of your love on every page.

To my sister-in-law for motivating and inspiring. Her belief that marriage and motherhood can never hold you back if your will power is strong enough deeply influenced me.

And finally, to every reader who joined Gatha on this journey—thank you for allowing this story to unfold in your imagination. I hope it awakens something within you, inspires exploration, and reminds you that sometimes the farthest places bring us closest to ourselves.

With all my love and gratitude,
Aishwarya Vikram Nadhe

Highlights of Manipur

Manipur offers delightful discoveries, from rolling hills and serene water bodies to the rarest flora and fauna. This enchanting land is also home to waterfalls that have skilfully remained hidden from the world for years. Experience a newfound appreciation for nature's beauty as you traverse the abundant, unexplored landscapes. Welcome to Manipur!

Below is a summary of the top reasons to visit this remarkable state:

Sr. No.	*PLACES*	*ABOUT*
1.	Kangla Fort	A step into the past
2.	Ima Keithel	Asia's largest market run entirely by women
3.	Manipur State Museum	Rich in cultural heritage and history
4.	Andro Village	Known for its pottery and the tempting Andro beer
5.	Shree Shree Govindajee Temple	A famous Vaishnavite Temple
6.	Loktak Lake	A renowned freshwater lake famous for its unique floating phumdis

7.	Keibul Lamjao National Park	The only floating National Park, home to the rare Sangai deer
8.	INA Memorial	The site where the first Indian flag was hoisted
9.	The Phangrei Mountain (Ukhrul)	A majestic hill range offering breathtaking panoramic views, with cultural significance
10.	The Legendary Shirui Hills (Ukhrul)	Famous for their beauty and home to the rare Shirui Lily flower, symbolizing Manipur's heritage
11.	Khangkhui Cave (Ukhrul)	An ancient limestone cave of archaeological importance, steeped in local folklore
12.	Mova Cave (Ukhrul)	Mysterious and unexplored, showcasing stunning limestone formations
13.	Tharon Cave (Tamen-glong)	A natural wonder echoing the secrets of ancient civilization, a testament to Manipur's prehis-toric past
14.	Barak River (Tamenglong)	A natural marvel
15.	Jiribam	The gateway to Manipur
16.	Churchandpur	Attractions include Geljang Re-sort, Zogam Tribal Museum in Tuiboung, Khuga Dam, Ngaloi Waterfalls, and Tonglon Caves
17.	Chandel	A tribal wonderland
18.	Tengnoupal	Visit the scenic India-Myanmar border

19.	Thoubal	Home to Kakching Garden, Khongjam War Memorial, Waithou Lake, and a thriving coffee culture
20.	Kangpokpi	A vibrant hill town perfect for adventurous treks to Koubru
21.	Senapati	Known for the Mao Gate, the cherry blossom experience in Mao Village, and the stone monoliths in Willong Khullen Village
22.	Luxmi Kitchen (Imphal)	A feast of flavours with local dishes like eromba, ooti, singju, kangsoi, nga atoiba thongba, and chak khao kheer
23.	Manipuri Dance	Features traditional dance forms like Ras Leela and Nat Sankirtan
24.	Manipuri Music	Features folk songs and traditional instruments like pena, pung, shankha, kartal, manjira, and bamboo flute
25.	Manipuri Art	Includes pottery, fabric made of lotus silk, handicrafts, cane / bamboo/wooden artefacts, and paintings
26.	Festivals	Sangai Festival, Shirui Lily Festival, Kang, Yaoshang, Cheiroba, Lai Hairoba, Heikru Hitongba, Ramzan Eid, Christmas, Chumpa, Emoinu, Ningol Chakhaoba, Kut, Gang Ngai, and Lui Ngai Ni

27.	Sports	Manipur is the birthplace of the modern polo game and other native sports. It is known as the nation's powerhouse of sports, producing renowned athletes like Mary Kom, Mirabai Chanu, Gingko Singh, Kunjarani Devi, and many more who have won medals in several international sports competitions

Explore the wonders of Manipur and discover all it has to offer!

How to Reach Manipur

You can travel to this beautiful 'Jewel Land' by air, train, or bus from various parts of India.

***By Air* -**
Imphal International Airport is located about 8 km from the heart of Imphal city and is well connected directly to major cities in India, including Delhi, Guwahati, Kolkata, Hyderabad, Mumbai, and major cities of the Northeastern states. Other cities are connected to Imphal via Kolkata, Guwahati, or Delhi.

***By Train* -**
There are no direct trains to Manipur. However, travellers can take a train to Guwahati or Dimapur (the nearest railway station) and then complete the journey by bus or by air.

***By Bus* -**
Numerous private bus services operate daily between Guwahati and Manipur on NH 27, NH 29, and NH 2 via Dimapur and Kohima. Private and state-run buses also connect Imphal to neighbouring cities like Dimapur, Kohima, Agartala, Aizawl, Itanagar, and Shillong.